the education publisher
for Scotland

T0337570

SNAP
REVISION
WRITING

Build your 4th Level English Skills

REVISE TRICKY TOPICS IN A SNAP

Alexandra Mattinson

Published by Leckie
An imprint of HarperCollins Publishers
Westerhill Road, Bishopbriggs
Glasgow G64 2QT

HarperCollins Publishers
Macken House, 39/40 Mayor Street Upper,
Dublin 1, D01 C9W8, Ireland

© HarperCollinsPublishers Limited 2022

ISBN 9780008528102

First published 2022

10 9 8 7 6 5 4 3 2 1

All rights reserved. No part of this publication
may be reproduced, stored in a retrieval
system, or transmitted, in any form or by any
means, electronic, mechanical, photocopying,
recording or otherwise, without the prior
permission of Collins.

British Library Cataloguing in Publication Data.
A CIP record of this book is available from
the British Library.

Commissioning Editors: Jenni Hall and
  Clare Souza
Author: Alexandra Mattinson
Project Editor: Peter Dennis
Typesetting: QBS Learning
Cover designer: Kneath Associates and
  Sarah Duxbury

Printed in the United Kingdom.

ACKNOWLEDGEMENTS
p.14, 26, Iain Crichton Smith, *The Telegram.*
From "The Red Door: The Complete English
Stories 1949-76" (Birlinn, 2017); p. 20, Iain
Crichton Smith *The Red Door.* From "The Red
Door: The Complete English Stories 1949-76"
(Birlinn, 2001); p. 35, Gina Berriault, *The Stone
Boy.* From "Women in their Beds: Thirty-Five
Stories" (Counterpoint, 2017); p. 49, E. B.
White, *Once More to the Lake.* From "Essays
of E. B. White" (Harper & Row, 1977); p. 50
Varaidzo, *A Guide to Being Black.* From "The
Good Immigrant" (Unbound, 2017).

The author and publisher are grateful to
the copyright holders for permission to use
quoted materials and images.

Every effort has been made to trace copyright
holders and obtain their permission for the
use of copyright material. The author and
publisher will gladly receive information
enabling them to rectify any error or omission
in subsequent editions. All facts are correct at
time of going to press.

MIX
Paper | Supporting
responsible forestry
FSC
www.fsc.org   FSC™ C007454

This book is produced from independently certified FSC™ paper
to ensure responsible forest management.

For more information visit: www.harpercollins.co.uk/green

Contents

ebook

To access the ebook version, visit collins.co.uk/ebooks and follow the step-by-step instructions.

Introduction

The writing element of your 4th level English course will give you a chance to be creative and will help you to prepare for the demands of the National 5 and Higher writing folio. At senior level, you are expected to work independently to produce a 'folio' (more than one piece) of writing. You may be asked to produce writing that discusses a topic you have researched (such as a discursive or a persuasive essay), or to plan and produce a creative piece of writing, for instance, a short story; a reflection of a personal experience; content for social media; a drama or television script; or poetry.

We will start by focusing on short story writing but remember: much of what you learn can be applied to all types of written content. You will also learn about persuasive techniques, which you can use to create social media content, an advertising brief or a persuasive essay.

By the end of this guide you will have written at least two pieces of extended writing: a short story and a persuasive essay, each with a word length of between 800 and 1300 words. This may seem a lot but it really isn't when you get going. You will also have completed a number of other tasks and these are no less important.

Read as many different examples of writing as you can. This will help you to learn about different styles and genres and is without question the best way to learn how to use language to engage an audience.

Some extracts are included in this book but before you start, it is advisable to have read the following short stories: *The Red Door* and *The Telegram* by Iain Crichton Smith. You will also need a journal to write down your ideas and have access to newspapers (either online or paper copies). To help familiarise yourself with persuasive and discursive writing styles, you should read as many magazine or newspaper articles from quality broadsheet newspapers as you can. Although not essential, it helps if you have use of a computer or laptop to type up your drafts.

Writing teaches us discipline; it improves our literacy skills; it teaches us to express our thoughts, feelings and opinions; and it provides an outlet for our creativity. We have to become effective readers and improve our understanding of content produced by others in order to improve our own writing.

You can start to improve your writing straight away by becoming an observer and learning about the world in which we live. Good writers do this. In the short story unit, you will develop your own characters and to do this, you will need to learn to become a close observer of the people around you – do be discreet! Watch how people interact (or don't), how they behave on their own (or around others), and try to describe their appearance in detail. Use a journal to jot down your findings and try to develop a blend of different characteristics to create a few strong characters that you could use in your stories. Get into the habit of using your journal so that you will have some strong ideas to draw upon.

In preparation for the discursive and persuasive styles of writing, try to improve your knowledge of a wide range of topics, such as environmental and political issues. Think about what is happening globally, nationally and locally. To help you with this task you can read news stories, watch the news and read good quality magazine articles.

It is important to be realistic about the amount of effort that goes into producing an effective piece of writing, no matter which subject you are writing for. Pupils often think about writing as being a one step process, but this is far from the truth: there are many different steps to creating effective written work. You will become a better writer immediately if you change your mindset and acknowledge that writing is a series of micro tasks that overlap with each other. Below is a list of the main steps involved in the writing process – these will be explored throughout the book.

Step 1. Research: look for and explore the ideas of others to inform or inspire our own work.

For example, in a science-based report or discursive topic, you may have to research facts and information. This research may involve a wide variety of approaches and it applies to all types of writing. For example, if you are creating a character who feels isolated or marginalised you could run an internet search on 'feeling isolated' for some ideas on how people might feel in real life if they were isolated – you could then apply this to your character. You could also research other texts that explore a theme of isolation to see how other authors have approached the topic. There are many different ways of note taking and you should find one that helps you.

Step 2. Planning: explore and experiment with all the different components (parts) that make up your story, such as plot, theme, character, structure, and setting (imaginative writing).

Include ideas from the research stage (this can be done using sticky notes, mind maps, sketches or lists). Structuring your narrative (experimenting with the order of your story) is really important and should always be planned for during these early stages. In an imaginative piece you could, for example, write the same story from the perspectives of two different characters, such as both the perpetrator of a crime and the victim. In a persuasive piece of writing, for example, you will want to make sure you have extended and developed your ideas and included topic sentences, linking words and phrases to ensure your arguments are presented in a sensible order and are easy to follow. Be experimental: the possibilities are endless.

Step 3. Development: bringing the work to life with detail and description. Here you will think about your use of language such as imagery, sentence structure and word choice.

Step 4. Re-writing or editing: turning your cygnet into a swan! If you have worked on a computer this will be easier. Think about the following during the edit stage: key ideas, structure and language. Your teacher or peers may have given you feedback. The re-writing or editing of your work is not simply just 'correcting mistakes'. This stage will be dictated by the time available but be aware that the more editing you do, the better the final results. Skip this step and you will be preparing to fail!

Final step! Close technical edit. You must now re-read your work (reading out loud is a good approach as it is easier to pick up little errors). Focus on making any final spelling, grammar or punctuation corrections. Never skip this step or do it quickly.

Task 1

Look back at the steps above. Beside the tasks that you find relatively easy, place a tick. The rest of the steps on the list will be your areas for improvement. Take a note of anything that you find challenging and beside each point, think of at least one way in which you are going to try and improve. See the table below for an example.

Steps I find easy	Steps I forget or find hard	Action plan	How will this help?
Example: editing stages, development and planning.	Research stage.	• Each week I choose one aspect of writing to research as an independent homework task. I will explore a wider variety of sources than I used to, such as: blogs, books, podcasts, YouTube videos and online articles. • To make sure I can access the research again quickly, I will record key points concisely. I will try the 'Cornell note taking system'. • I will use my research points in my writing work.	I will have plenty of content to include in my plan and to use for developing my ideas. My work will show depth and insight. I will improve my research skills, which will help in all of my subject areas and in life beyond school.

Task 2

Learn to take notes properly. Research the Cornell method of note taking and use it to practice. Summarise the instructions presented to you, using the Cornell method. Keep your summary handy as an example. This will be helpful in all of your subjects.

Key elements of imaginative writing

Different forms of writing share common traits. For example, a script for TV might require a specific layout to instruct the director where and when the action takes place. However, in short story writing (which is usually continuous prose) the location and time of any action is written as part of the story and is not just an instruction. Many types or forms of writing share a common set of 'ingredients'. This analogy works well because once you know which different elements work together to make up an effective story, you can combine them in any way you wish. Your 'ingredients' go into a melting pot (plan) and come out as an individual story. That's the magic.

The following is an overview of the main points to consider when creating a short story, which, for our purpose, should be around 800–1300 well planned, well crafted and thoroughly edited words. Each point MUST be considered in detail if your story is to be effective. The points are expanded upon later in the guide.

1. **Genre**
   For this purpose, we will refer to genre as types of texts that we can group together and identify as sharing similar typical traits. For example, the science fiction genre may include time travel, teleportation, extra-terrestrial beings or a parallel universe. Spend some time researching your chosen genre as each will employ a typical set of expectations or rules. As a further example, a story in the suspense genre may feature a number of plot twists; a few subtle clues (often only evident after the ending reveal); and they may employ a cliffhanger to finish. Once you have a set of genre expectations to consider, you can break them, twist them or combine them to shock, surprise or delight your reader.

2. **Theme**
   A theme is **a key idea** explored within the text such as: love, relationships, guilt, identity, gender or loss. For instance, the main theme in *Winnie the Pooh* is the importance of long-lasting friendships. You will be familiar with the significance of theme from texts you have studied in English so far. A story that has been created from an interesting theme will always feel more genuine than one that has not. It is a great place to start planning. Themes relate to the world in which we live and are what make us human. Remember though, it is your treatment of and representation of that theme that becomes important in the end.

3. **Mood, atmosphere and tone**
   These are certainly literary terms that you should be aware of although they are often confused. The mood of the story is really the atmosphere. To create a mood means to create a sense of, for example, fear or drama. If your purpose is to entertain your readers and you have chosen a horror genre, they would expect to be scared or fearful at points throughout your story. Remember too that **moods can change** throughout the story – this will keep it varied and interesting.

   Much of your planning time will be spent creating mood or atmosphere.

   Remember that audience engagement is key. If you ever had a comment from a teacher that suggested that your story was 'not engaging enough'; 'a little flat' or 'needed to be brought to life', it is very likely that you needed to add more atmosphere. A word of warning: pupils often rely on word choice, imagery, sentence structure and punctuation to create an effective atmosphere and of course these are very important. However, without first having an effective plot (or storyline, see point 7 below), even the most "atmospheric" piece of writing is very unlikely to ever be truly engaging. There is an oft used saying: you can't make a silk purse out of a sow's ear. Get the basic idea right first.

Tone reflects more the writer's attitude towards the story. So, if you were passionately disagreeing with a topic, such as "the use of phones in class", you may be quite **scathing** or **angry** in your **tone.**

4. Characterisation
This refers to the representations of the people or objects in your story that bring it to life. The majority of characters in stories are human although using inanimate objects or animals as your characters (often hinted at throughout but revealed at the end) can be an amazing way to engage your readers. Your characters will bring your themes to life. For example, two characters who did not get along could reveal a theme of conflict and disharmony within relationships. Characters must be fully developed – see the chapter on characterisation to help with this.

5. Dialogue
Although technically part of characterisation, it is added here separately as many pupils feel the need to 'script' the whole story through the voice of the character. This results in a 'he said: 'she said' style of writing which is repetitive and boring at best. There other ways to reveal plot, for example through actions – see further sections. On the other hand, good dialogue used effectively, can reveal much about your character, such as the accent and phrasing of the dialogue can be very important. Dialogue done well can help the characters come to life. Unfinished sentences, hesitations, deliberate repetitions can help the work feel much more realistic. You can have a great deal of fun working with character dialogue.

6. Setting
Don't underestimate this part of the story. The time and place of your story should be evident all the way through, not over and done with in the first sentence. Setting should be developed and will support your theme. A detailed description of setting and a considered reference to the time in which the story is set, will help you create engagement. Push the boundaries of your setting choices: an unusual setting for the chosen characters creates conflict, which in turn keeps the audience interested.

7. Language
The way you manipulate language techniques will essentially be the make or break of your finished piece. It is no good having a great theme and brilliant characters in your head if you can't express that through word choice, sentence structure and original imagery. This is another reason to read more and to take notes of any language features or word choices that you love.

8. Plot
For the purpose of this book (which reflects the need of the curriculum) we will think of plot as the storyline. It will be a combination of all of the above. In essence: the story. In a short story you must be realistic about what you can achieve and how much you can include. You are not writing a novel; you do not need a cast of thousands; you do not need to fill in every little detail; you do not even need to complete the story. Some of the

best short stories end on a cliffhanger and leave much to the imagination of the reader. It does have to make sense: be realistic about word count limitations and keep it real.

9. **Narration style**

This refers to the way that you choose to tell the story and who you want to tell it to! Once you have decided on the story, you will have to decide who is going to narrate it and most importantly – why. The narrator could be one or two characters from the story (perhaps to portray particular slant or bias), or a voice that has nothing to do with the story itself in order to provide a more neutral account. You may combine both – use more than one narrator in your story. You will also have to consider whether you are telling it in past or present tense and you will have reasons for your selection. There are different types of narrator – see pages (36–40).

10. **Structure**

This is the way you put your story together: where you start and end your story and the order in which you place everything in between. Changing the order of these points will change your story completely and a clever, considered structure is a very effective way of adding impact and making your story stand out. Pay attention to the chapter on narrative structure if you need help with this.

> ### Task 3
>
> Short imaginative task
>
> Pick a theme that interests you, such as loss, isolation or new beginnings. Now choose a tone that you may not normally expect to be representative of this theme and write one paragraph about how you could tell the story. Remember, this is just an exercise designed to help you push the boundaries of your imagination.
>
> **Example**: Theme – the struggles of war. Unusual tone – comedy. Summary – a group of middle-aged and ill-equipped men are charged with bringing order in a time of chaos, with hilarious consequences.

Genre

In the last chapter you learned that genre is a 'type' – a useful way to group together different sorts of texts (or in our case 'stories'). Each genre of writing will have its own set of expectations (or rules) that writers have developed and have relied upon throughout history. Identifying and using the rules of a genre can help you to structure your own writing (arrange the different parts of your story in an effective order). It is important to note that you might have to mix and match genre conventions for some of the stories you want to create. Don't worry, it is not an exact science (see the next chapter for more information).

By considering these commonly used rules, you will be helping your audience to better understand the key points of your story. They will be familiar with the genre and recognise certain aspects because you made them easily identifiable. Please note that such predictability is not always a good thing. If, in the research stage of your writing you experimented with different blends of genre, your final piece could be very engaging for the audience as your story will become harder to predict. Challenging the expectations of your audience is a very good thing!

Genre conventions?

Stories of a particular genre may explore similar themes; be written in a particular style; share some common settings; and may contain many of the same character types. **See below for a worked example.**

Genre type	Typical characters	Typical settings	Typical theme	Typical plot points	Typical ending
The Western	Hero, victim and villain. Often: Native Americans, nomadic cowboys, gunfighters, bandits, bounty hunters, beautiful but tragic women in need of rescue, outlaws and gamblers.	American Old West. 19thC (the latter half). Often set in harsh wilderness, with hostile and desolate landscapes such as: deserts, mountains, ranches, small towns and saloons.	Survival, revenge, bravery, righteousness, and isolation. For example, a protagonist being exiled from their society.	Centres around conflict. Often the protagonist will face a series of struggles, overthrow the antagonist and save the victim. Revenge shown by chase and pursuit.	Revenge and retribution, usually a shootout.

Can you see how an idea such as the one in the table above would be challenging to complete within the restrictions of a short story? If you are interested in the western genre, why not try to write the opening chapter of a longer story – this allows you to try many of the above conventions. You could also write a **dramatic monologue** from the protagonist's point of view as they reflect on a situation of your choice. This allows you to develop characterisation whilst still sticking to the genre which will be made clear to the audience as certain key aspects are revealed.

Note: A dramatic monologue is a piece of writing or a speech that presents the thoughts of just one character to the audience. This way of writing offers insight about the character to the readers.

Task 4

1. Using the grid above, try to fill in the columns for the following genres: a ghost story, a suspense story, a thriller, a sci-fi story. Remember to research the common traits of the genre.
2. Pick either one of the plots below (or one of your own) and answer the following questions. Which genres do you think the plots belong to and what are some of the conventions of those genres? You will have to research online before completing this task. See the Answer section at the back of the book for suggested answers.
   a. *A young girl studying at college for a better future has to deal with a number of social difficulties such as: poverty, looking after younger siblings, alcoholism and drug use in her immediate family.*
   b. *Two friends set out on a planned day out to the city but encounter several incidents on the way including: the mysterious disappearance of the train driver as he unexpectedly disembarks at a station on the way, and an unnerving moment when a taxi driver appears to already know their names and exactly where they are going.*

Genre 2

We have learned about the importance of considering genre conventions and how you can surprise your reader through 'mixing and matching' different conventions. In this chapter we will look more closely at blending genres. But before we continue it is worth considering the purpose of genre and the link to audience.

A word on audience and the importance of genre

Your readers are very familiar with common genres and once they have identified some common traits, such as little clues leading up to a reveal in a ghost story, they will start to predict the ending. That is where you can change things around and surprise them with a mix of two different genres. If your story is harder to predict, your audience will be more engaged as they try to work out the plot and hopefully, be surprised by the ending having enjoyed your original story.

Why does audience matter? You are writing for an audience – in this case probably a teacher and as you move to your senior phase, an examiner from your examination board – the Scottish Qualifications Authority (SQA). You have your work cut out because both your teacher and examiner have already read a great many essays in their career and have seen it all: the good, the bad and the ugly. **How** are you going to engage them? You have to make them actively involved in the reading process. *Give them something to do* (such as working out clues or working out two different plot strands that come together in an unexpected way). **Make them work**! If you give away the story from the beginning, you cannot possibly expect them to be engaged.

A good place to start, would be to **consider the purpose** of the piece. Imaginative writing is largely created to entertain a reader but you need a secondary purpose. Do you want to scare, shock, surprise, make your reader think about a particular theme, make them laugh or a combination of above? Make this decision at the start then work hard to make that happen from your first word to your last.

What can produce a very original story is to think about mixing genres as your readers expect one thing but you deliver another. Try this now: you will be well on your way to engaging your audience!

 Task 5

1. Write a short paragraph that considers the following questions in preparation for writing a short story.
    How do you want your reader to feel, or think, both as they read and when they have finished reading your story?

2. With your answers to the above in mind, complete the next task.

a. Below is a list of possible genres and some more obscure sub-genres! Read through the list and make a note of the ones you might like to use in your short story. You might have to research some examples first. The list is not exhaiustive – do add to it if you can.

Children's literature. Thriller. Science Fiction. Romance. Realism. Comedy. Horror. Fairytale. Fantasy. Tragedy. Folktale. Myth. Legend. Crime. Detective. Allegory. Adventure. Autobiography. Gothic fiction. Melodrama. Mystery. Parody. Vampire fiction. Climate fiction. History/Alternate history. Contemporary. Paranormal. Dark fantasy. Superhero. Sword and Sorcery. Psychological thriller. Private detective. Military. Time Travel. Apocalyptic/post-apocalyptic. Colonisation. Cyberpunk or post human. Dystopia and utopia. Galactic Empire. Lost Worlds. Spyfi. Conspiracy. Disaster. Espionage. Forensic. Medical. Religious. Western. Alternate or parallel universe.

b. Now have a go at mixing two examples together to create an interesting blend of two genres while all the time thinking of the purpose of the story and how you want you reader to feel. For each example write down a brief idea for a story. Aim for at least five examples. When you find one that you think works well, do a little research to find the conventions of both genres. The table below will help you.

You don't have to include all of the suggested conventions in your story – just what works for you. Such examples could be: *children's story + crime*; **realism +** *horror*; *western + comedy* or **fairytales + thriller**.

Genre types	Typical characters	Typical settings	Common themes	Typical plot points	Common endings

Short story example: The Telegram

The best way to become a good writer is to become a great reader. Before you start working through the short story work that follows, take time out to carefully read *The Telegram* by Iain Crichton Smith. The story is set in a small Scottish village during World War Two. It has only two main characters yet through them we are left in no doubt of the devastating impact war has on a community. There are some questions for you to consider at the end of the story.

The two women – one fat and one thin – sat at the window of the thin woman's house drinking tea and looking down the road which ran through the village. They were like two birds, one a fat domestic bird perhaps, the other more aquiline, more gaunt, or, to be precise, more like a buzzard.

It was wartime and though the village appeared quiet, much had gone on in it. Reverberations from a war fought far away had reached it: many of its young men had been killed, or rather drowned, since nearly all of them had joined the navy, and their ships had sunk in seas which they had never seen except on maps which hung on the walls of the local school which they all had at one time or another unwillingly attended. One had been drowned on a destroyer after a leave during which he had told his family that he would never come back again. (Or at least that was the rumour in the village which was still, as it had always been, a superstitious place.) Another had been drowned during the pursuit of the *Bismarck*.

What the war had to do with them the people of the village did not know. It came on them as a strange plague, taking their sons away and then killing them, meaninglessly, randomly. They watched the road often for the telegrams.

The telegrams were brought to the houses by the local elder who, clad in black, would walk along the road and then stop at the house to which the telegram was directed. People began to think of the telegram as a strange missile pointed at them from abroad. They did not know what to associate it with, certainly not with God, but it was a weapon of some kind, it picked a door and entered it, and left desolation just like any other weapon.

The two women who watched the street were different, not only physically but socially. For the thin woman's son was a sub-lieutenant in the Navy while the fat woman's son was only an ordinary seaman. The fat woman's son had to salute the thin woman's son. One got more pay than the other, and wore better uniform. One had been at university and had therefore become an officer, the other had left school at the age of fourteen.

When they looked out the window they could see cows wandering lazily about, but little other movement. The fat woman's cow used to eat the thin woman's washing and she was looking out for it but she couldn't see it. The thin woman was not popular in the village. She was an incomer from another village and had only been in this one for thirty years or so. The fat woman had lived in the village all her days; she was a native. Also the thin woman was ambitious: she had sent her son to university though she only had a widow's pension of ten shillings a week.

As they watched they could see at the far end of the street the tall man in black clothes carrying in his hand a piece of yellow paper. This was a bare village with little colour and therefore the yellow was both strange and unnatural.

The fat woman said: 'It's Macleod again.' 'I wonder where he's going today.'

They were both frightened for he could be coming to their house. And so they watched him and as they watched him they spoke feverishly as if by speaking continually and watching his every move they would be able to keep from themselves whatever plague he was bringing. The thin woman said:

'Don't worry, Sarah, it won't be for you. Donald only left home last week.'

'You don't know,' said the fat woman, 'you don't know.' And then she added without thinking, 'It's different for the officers.'

'Why is it different for the officers?' said the thin woman in an even voice without taking her eyes from the black figure.

'Well, I just thought they're better off,' said the fat woman in a confused tone, 'they get better food and they get better conditions.'

'They're still on the ship,' said the thin woman who was thinking that the fat woman was very stupid. But then most of them were: they were large, fat and lazy. Most of them could have better afforded to send their sons and daughters to university but they didn't want to be thought of as snobbish.

'They are that,' said the fat woman. 'But your son is educated,' she added irrelevantly. Of course her son didn't salute the thin woman's son if they were both home on leave at the same time. It had happened once they had been. But naturally there was the uneasiness.

'I made sacrifices to have my son educated,' said the thin woman. 'I lived on a pension of ten shillings a week. I was in nobody's debt. More tea?'

'No thank you,' said the fat woman. 'He's passed Bessie's house. That means it can't be Roddy. He's safe.'

For a terrible moment she realised that she had hoped that the elder would have turned in at Bessie's house. Not that she had anything against Bessie or Roddy. But still one thought of one's own family first.

The thin woman continued remorselessly as if she were pecking away at something she had pecked at for many years. 'The teacher told me to send Iain to University. He came to see me. I had no thought of sending him before he came. "Send your son to university," he said to me. "He's got a good head on him." And I'll tell you, Sarah, I had to save every penny. Ten shillings isn't much. When did you see me with good clothes in the church?'

'That's true,' said the fat woman absently. 'We have to make sacrifices.' It was difficult to know what she was thinking of-the whale meat or the saccharines? Or the lack of clothes? Her mind was vague and diffused except when she was thinking about herself.

The thin woman continued: 'Many's the night I used to sit here in this room and knit clothes for him when he was young. I even knitted trousers for him. And for all I know he may marry an

English girl and where will I be? He might go and work in England. He was staying in a house there at Christmas. He met a girl at a dance and he found out later that her father was a mayor. I'm sure she smokes and drinks. And he might not give me anything after all I've done for him.'

'Donald spends all his money,' said the fat woman. 'He never sends me anything. When he comes home on leave he's never in the house. But I don't mind. He was always like that. Meeting strange people and buying them drinks. It's his nature and he can't go against his nature. He's passed the Smiths. That means Tommy's all right.'

There were only another three houses before he would reach her own, and then the last one was the one where she was sitting.

'I think I'll take a cup of tea,' she said. And then, 'I'm sorry about the cow. 'But no matter how you tried you never could like the thin woman. She was always putting on airs. Mayor indeed. Sending her son to university. Why did she want to be better than anyone else? Saving and scrimping all the time. And everybody said that her son wasn't as clever as all that. He had failed some of his exams too. Her own Donald was just as clever and could have gone to university but he was too fond of fishing and being out with the boys.

As she drank her tea her heart was beating and she was frightened and she didn't know what to talk about and yet she wanted to talk. She liked talking, after all what else was there to do? But the thin woman didn't gossip much. *You* couldn't feel at ease with her, you had the idea all the time that she was thinking about something else.

The thin woman came and sat down beside her.

'Did you hear,' said the fat woman, 'that Malcolm Mackay was up on a drunken charge? He smashed his car, so they say. It was in the black-out.'

'I didn't hear that,' said the thin woman.

'It was coming home last night with the meat. He had it in the van and he smashed it at the burn. But they say he's all right. I don't know how they kept him out of the war. They said it was his heart but there was nothing wrong with his heart. Everyone knows it was influence. What's wrong with his heart if he can drink and smash a car?'

The thin woman drank her tea very delicately. She used to be away on service a long time before she was married and she had a dainty way of doing things. She sipped her tea, her little finger elegantly curled in an irritating way.

'Why do you keep your finger like that?' said the fat woman suddenly.

'Like what?' The fat woman demonstrated.

'Oh, it was the way I saw the guests drinking tea in the hotels when I was on service. They always drank like that.'

'He's passed the Stewarts, said the fat woman. Two houses to go. They looked at each other wildly. It must be one of them. Surely. They could see the elder quite clearly now, walking very stiff, very upright, wearing his black hat. He walked in a stately dignified manner, eyes straight ahead of him.

'He's proud of what he's doing,' said the fat woman suddenly. 'You'd think he was proud of it. Knowing before anyone else. And he himself was never in the war.'

'Yes,' said the thin woman, 'it gives him a position.' They watched him. They both knew him well. He was a stiff, quiet man who kept himself to himself, more than ever now. He didn't mix with people and he always carried the Bible into the pulpit for the minister.

'They say his wife had one of her fits again,' said the fat woman viciously. He had passed the Murrays. The next house was her own. She sat perfectly still. Oh, pray God it wasn't hers. And yet it must be hers. Surely it must be hers. She had dreamt of this happening, her son drowning in the Atlantic ocean, her own child whom she had reared, whom she had seen going to play football in his green jersey and white shorts, whom she had seen running home from school. She could see him drowning but she couldn't make out the name of the ship. She had never seen a really big ship and what she imagined was more like the mailboat than a cruiser. Her son couldn't drown out there for no reason that she could understand. God couldn't do that to people. It was impossible. God was kinder than that. God helped you in your sore trouble. She began to mutter a prayer over and over. She said it quickly like the Catholics, O God save my son O God save my son O God save my son. She was ashamed of prattling in that way as if she was counting beads but she couldn't stop herself, and on top of that she would soon cry. She knew it and she didn't want to cry in front of that woman, that foreigner. It would be weakness. She felt the arm of the thin woman around her shoulders, the thin arm, and it was like first love, it was like the time Murdo had taken her hand in his when they were coming home from the dance, such an innocent gesture, such a spontaneous gesture. So unexpected, so strange, so much a gift. She was crying and she couldn't look...

'He has passed your house,' said the thin woman in a distant firm voice, and she looked up. He was walking along and he had indeed passed her house. She wanted to stand up and dance all round the kitchen, all fifteen stone of her, and shout and cry and sing a song but then she stopped. She couldn't do that. How could she do that when it must be the thin woman's son? There was no other house. The thin woman was looking out at the elder, her lips pressed closely together, white and bloodless; Where had she learnt that self control? She wasn't crying or shaking. She was looking out at something she had always dreaded but she wasn't going to cry or surrender or give herself away to anyone.

And at that moment the fat woman saw. She saw the years of discipline, she remembered how thin and unfed and pale the thin woman had always looked, how sometimes she had had to borrow money, even a shilling to buy food. She saw what it must have been like to be a widow bringing up a son in a village not her own. She saw it so clearly that she was astounded. It was as if she had an extra vision, as if the air itself brought the past with all its details nearer. The number of times the thin woman had been ill and people had said that she was weak and useless. She looked down at the thin woman's arm. It was so shrivelled, and dry.

And the elder walked on. A few yards now till he reached the plank. But the thin woman hadn't cried. She was steady and still, her lips still compressed, sitting upright in her chair. And, miracle of miracles, the elder passed the plank and walked straight on.

They looked at each other. What did it all mean? Where was the elder going, clutching his telegram in his hand, walking like a man in a daze? There were no other houses so where was he going? They drank their tea in silence, turning away from each other. The fat woman said, 'I must be going.' They parted for the moment without speaking. The thin woman still sat at the window looking out. Once or twice the fat woman made as if to turn back as if she had something to say, some message to pass on, but she didn't. She walked away.

It wasn't till later that night that they discovered what had happened. The elder had a telegram directed to himself, to tell him of the drowning of his own son. He should never have seen it just like that, but there had been a mistake at the post office, owing to the fact that there were two boys in the village with the same name. His walk through the village was a somnambulistic wandering. He didn't want to go home and tell his wife what had happened. He was walking along not knowing where he was going when later he was stopped half way to the next village. Perhaps he was going in search of his son. Altogether he had walked six miles. The telegram was crushed in his fingers and so sweaty that they could hardly make out the writing.

Task 6

There are several main themes in *The Telegram*, such as the destructiveness of war and living as an outsider in a rural environment.

1. List as many examples as you can from the text that highlight these themes.
   For each example make a comment explaining how it is effective in exploring that theme. Note any techniques such as: word choice, imagery, conflict between characters, conflict between character and setting, etc.

The build up of tension is central to the effectiveness of the ending of the story.

2. Draw a timeline of key events in *The Telegram* to help you see how tension can be created. Consider the opening, development, climax, falling action and resolution.

   > Irony can be used as a clever twist in the ending of a story and the climax of *The Telegram* is a perfect illustration of this. Irony is shown here when it turns out that the telegram bearer is carrying the news of his own son's death. It is important because it is a poignant (emotional) reminder that war affects everyone. Irony is a contrast between what we expect to happen and what actually happens in the story. Using irony your short story can help you to convey an idea in a very impactful way.

3. Try re-writing the ending of *The Telegram* in a different way.

The thin woman in the story has endured great sacrifice to ensure her son has the best start possible.

4. Plan your own story where a character shows great sacrifice.
   a. Explain the situation
   b. Explain the feelings of the character in your story. Do they feel bitter? Regret? Are they selfless? In what ways has the sacrifice affected them? Try to write at least one paragraph that could be developed into a story at a later date.

5. Write a paragraph that summarises a significant moment in the life of a character. This is something that you could later develop into a short story.

Now write a paragraph for a significant moment in your own life. It doesn't have to be tragic, it just has to be important to you in some way.

Theme

You have already learned that 'theme' is central to your story and it is preferable that you explore this aspect of story writing at the planning stage. By writing through the eyes of your chosen theme you will end up with far more depth in your story. A well written narrative will most likely touch on one or two themes.

Remember: theme is simply a broad, identifiable key message (about a particular aspect of life) that runs through a story and provides both focus and meaning. It is usually **inferred** by the reader, not stated.

For example:

- **Individual versus society** – a story revolving around a main character who struggles as an outsider: *The Red Door* by Iain Crichton Smith;

- **Coming of age** – experience of a young person leading to loss of innocence or change: *Little Women* by Louisa May Alcott or *The Catcher in the Rye* by JD Salinger;

- **Power and corruption** – *Macbeth* by William Shakespeare or *The Hunger Games* by Suzanne Collins;

- **Survival** – *Life of Pi* by Yann Martel;

- **The destructive consequence of prejudice** – *To Kill A Mockingbird by Harper Lee*.

In the young adult genre, the themes presented are often important life lessons associated with the transition from childhood to adulthood, such as: overcoming adversity; forming an identity; living and working in harmony with others; loss of innocence; learning from your elders; or facing fears. Can you think of any others?

Some great examples of young adult novels are: *The Lion the Witch and the Wardrobe*: C. S. Lewis; *The Fault in Our Stars*: John Green; *The Perks of Being a Wallflower*: Steven Chbosky; *The Outsiders*: S. E. Hinton; *Little Women*: Louisa May Alcott; and *The Diary of a Young Girl*: Anne Frank. A quick internet search will reveal a wealth of young adult titles to suit all tastes. Exploring and enjoying the work of the writers and understanding how they explore or reveal important issues is the best way to learn about themes (and the craft of story writing in general).

Task 7

1. What themes do you think are central to the following stories?
   - Cinderella
   - Snow White
   - Brave
   - Shrek

2. Read the extract below from *The Red Door* by Iain Crichton Smith. This story, like many of his others, is relatively uncomplicated and this makes it easier to pick out the themes. If you can find a copy of the full story then you can try the same questions with the whole piece.

At the start of the story we learn that the main character 'Murdo', who lived in a traditional Highland village, was well liked, never did anything out of the ordinary and awoke after the night of Halloween to find his door painted red.

...<u>It certainly singled him out</u>. The door was as red as the winter sun he saw in the sky.

<u>Murdo had never in his life done anything unusual</u>. Indeed because he was a bachelor <u>he felt it necessary</u> that he <u>should be as like the other villagers as possible</u>. He read the Daily Record <u>as they did</u>, after dinner he slept by the fire <u>as they did</u>, he would converse with his neighbour while hammering a post into the ground. He would even play draughts with them sometimes.

<u>Nevertheless there were times</u> he felt that <u>there was more to life than that</u>.... At times too he would <u>find it difficult to get up in the morning</u> but would lie in a pleasant half dream looking up at the ceiling. <u>He would say to himself</u>, 'After all <u>I have nothing to get up for</u> really. I could if I liked, stay in bed all day and all night <u>and none would know the difference</u>. I used to do this when I was a child. <u>Why can't I do this now?</u> ...

Complete the following table for all of the underlined pieces of text in the extract. The first one has been done for you.

An important quote that you have identified	What is being suggested by this quote and how?	Potential theme
'It certainly singled him out'.	One of his first thoughts, despite the bizarre situation he found himself in, was that he may be seen to be different to the other villagers. Interestingly, is unclear whether this is a good or bad thing at this point. This short emphatic sentence is straight to the point and gives us a glimpse into his thoughts.	The reader is prompted to question the pressure many of us feel in order to conform to the expectations of others.

Exploring this story further

If you have access to the entire story, you should read it several times over and try to find more examples of the themes that you have identified above. Try to look at HOW the themes are explored. For example: is it through Murdo's character, thoughts or actions? The actions of others? The setting? Various plot points? If you do not have access to the above story, any other short story will work. *Please remember you are doing this in order to better understand how to apply theme to your own short stories.*

3. **A more challenging task!**

   Complete the above task for the short story *The Telegram* (see page 14) by completing the table below. Firstly, identify a list of key themes and then choose quotes that you think explore, or hint at, those themes. Copy the table below to help you. Remember to consider character, setting, plot points, structure and language.

   Example:

A list of all the themes you can identify in the story *The Telegram*.	An important quote that you have identified.	What is being suggested by this quote and how?	Potential theme
The idea that the horrors of war are far reaching and can affect a great many people.	'taking their sons away and then killing them, meaninglessly, randomly'.	That 'the war' devoured the men from the village in a ongoing, brutal and senseless way. 'Their sons' reminds us that entire families have been devastated.	It highlights clearly the idea that war is merciless and doesn't discriminate. It affects everyone (or the effect of war is devastating).

Look at the table headings:

- What you think the main themes are?
- Give examples of quotes (or examples of key events) that you think explore the theme. Explain what you think is being suggested and how.

Complete the table for each key theme in *The Telegram* on pages 14–18.

Task 8: Writing Task

Create a simple plan of potential ideas. Think about themes you feel you can explore in your own writing (through character, plot, setting etc.).

The following table may help you. Try to complete at least five examples and then choose the one that you feel would work best as a short story.

TIP When you have finished, highlight all of the key vocabulary – these are your power words and should help you create tone. (See below.)

What issues are really important to you and/or your peers?

Fear for the future of our planet.

What themes could you narrow this down to?

Mistrust of government (what are they doing to help/how did they let it get so bad)

Global unity (affects all species)

Feeling powerless (how can this be fixed now)

Survival

Humans versus nature.

Write one or two sentences to give the premise of a story that could explore these themes.

N.B. The 'premise' of your story is a brief statement of the idea.

Two characters from the same food chain are united through their fear for a future that will destroy their planet.

Tale of survival told in 1ˢᵗ person from the perspective of two different animals experiencing the same issues.

If the plant life can't survive, the small organisms that the fish eat can't survive. If the fish can't survive the other animals can't either. The food chain is altered. Species will disappear.

What types of characters would work well with this theme? Think of conflicting characters.

What is the clear message you want to give the audience?

How do you want the audience to feel? Why?

Two characters, although not immediately obvious, are animals (normally predator and prey) affected by environmental issues.

For example, the otter – reveals her struggles as she tries to rear her young on a stretch of water with dangerously deteriorating fish stocks.

A fish trying to survive and watching her own young fail in waters devoid of life.

Message: environmental issues affect us all and change the natural function of the whole ecosystem. This changes the way the world works.

I want the audience to feel shocked, frustrated and sad. So that they take action in some small way.

Where could you set the story? Think of challenging your characters to reveal the theme.

Harsh and barren waterways of the Scottish countryside. Normally teaming with life they are now home to very little.

Any other supporting notes to help you, including any challenges that you may have to think about.

This would work well as a monologue of a snapshot in time from the perspectives of the two different species. I will give my animals some human characteristics because this will ensure my audience feels a strong sense of empathy and regret.

I may have to think about the ending. I want to keep it subtle but impactful with a really clear message. Is the natural order of food chain flipped as the fish feed on a larger animal? The audience may assume, sadly, that this is perhaps the body of a young otter that has succumbed to starvation. I would want to be sensitive but impactful. I wouldn't need to reveal the ending thus encouraging engagement as the audience has to work out the ending.

Which genre would work well?

Elements of realism as mothers worry about a desperate situation – the survival and demise of their young.

Potential for some elements of adventure set in a postapocalyptic landscape -a desperately barren and harsh landscape where survival seems against the odds.

Look at the words highlighted in the task above. These are key (power) words that have naturally emerged.

Word choice is one way to create tone (feeling) or atmosphere in your work. Other words for tone could be 'ambiance' or 'vibe'. What sort of tone do you think would emerge from the highlighted words above?

You may have chosen 'desolate' or 'dark' for example (try to think of more). When you have identified the tone in your own idea (it is important to keep returning to your plan in order to remind yourself) you will have to look at ways of developing that tone through more word choice, imagery, sentence structure, punctuation, selection of plot points, the structure of the story, the setting and all the other elements discussed in this guide.

How to develop great characters

Developing your characters is one of the most exciting parts of story writing. However, creating believable characters can be quite a challenge. For a successful assessment at 4th level and beyond, you will have to show that you have worked hard on this aspect of your story.

Look at the follow assessment criteria from the 4th level Experiences and Outcomes.

Having explored and experimented with the narrative structures which writers use to create texts in different genres, I can: create convincing relationships, actions and dialogue for my characters. ENG 4-31a

The assessment criteria asks that we explore the following aspects of characterisation:

Aspect of characterisation	Example
1. Convincing relationships (believable)	*How do your characters interact with others? Are they confident, shy, stand-offish, prefer to blend in to the background, awkward, wary of others, loving or cold and distanced. How do others respond to them? Maybe they are a little misunderstood.* **TIP**: *to make it more convincing you could think about why they act this way.*
2. Actions	*The actions of your characters will largely depend on the plot but key here is to think about the type of person they are. How might they react in any given situation? They, like any person, are driven by their values and beliefs and this is based on their previous experiences of life.* **TIP**: *Show don't tell.*
3. Dialogue	*Use sparingly and for impact. Poor use of dialogue often ruins an otherwise good story. See below.*

The key criteria from the SQA N5 general marking guidelines for imaginative writing require that you must demonstrate: *'strong creative qualities and a skilful command of the genre'*. This could be demonstrated by developing original, strong and believable characters and keeping that characterisation going from the beginning to the end of your story.

In order to make your characters **well rounded**, you will have to consider the following:

- the **way they act**
- the way **others act around them**
- **what they say** and **what others say about them** (including the narrator)
- their **appearance**.

To work out how your characters will act you have to consider what their **back story** is (this doesn't have to be included in the story, it just helps you work out the way they will act in certain situations). Character actions, well written, suggest who they are on a larger scale.

Imagine yourself as a character in the story of your own life. Fill in the following table. Try to be honest. Be as detailed as you can in each answer.

How would your friends describe you?	How would you describe yourself?	What are your greatest fears?	Do you ever behave in a way that you wish you didn't? Why do you think this might be?	Describe your appearance in detail. Add in the way you like to dress if you wish.	What do you think you sound like when you speak? Think about the vocabulary you use, your accent the pitch of your voice and the speed at which you speak. How confident is your speech?

The following is a list of common character problems. As you start planning your own story, use this as a checklist to avoid these pitfalls. It is important to note that sometimes rules are broken with great results. These are general guidelines that may help you with common errors.

Problem	Why this could be an issue	The fix
The main character/ characters aren't developed.	You are limited by word count so you won't have time to develop and show off your characterisation skills if you have too many characters. You will not be able to show any depth to your characters. They will not be convincing.	Make sure you focus on one or two characters. Don't let the minor characters take over. Brainstorm various aspects of the character's personality and situation.
There are too many characters.	The story will be diluted (weak) if you have a cast of thousands. You won't be able to create strong conflict, drama or insight (understanding of your characters) and this will definitely be an issue.	Make sure each of your characters has a role in the story. Do not just add them because you think you have to. You may only need one. Ask yourself why each character is there.

Problem	Why this could be an issue	The fix
Your characters are too 'talky'.	Action is revealed through too much character dialogue or basic 'telling by the story' narrator (for example if written in the 3rd person). Please note: writing in the style of a dramatic monologue (in which only one person is speaking rather than an interaction) would be an exception.	You must try to reveal plot through showing the actions and reactions of the characters, rather than allowing them (or the narrator) to explain how they feel. Use imagery – a picture is worth a thousand words. Remember that very well-crafted dialogue can be extremely effective.
Characterisation is weak.	You have just dropped a character into the story without enough planning and research. Your character most likely reacts to the events in an unconvincing way. We don't really care about them because you have created an unsympathetic character. They get lost in the background – probably taking your theme with them!	Research and develop your characters beforehand. You do not need to explain their backstory from within the story, you can hint at it. Time spent on this step will not be wasted. Consider how the character can be a vehicle to carry your theme.

The best way to learn how to write good characters is to read the work of good writers. Look again at the following extract from the short story *The Telegram*. The whole backstory of one of the main characters is revealed through simple **observations** from another character. We do not need pages explaining how hard life had been for her. It is exposition (description) but it is summarised **concisely** through several sentences.

> And at that moment the fat woman saw. She saw the years of discipline, she remembered how thin and unfed and pale the thin woman had always looked, how sometimes she had had to borrow money, even a shilling to buy food. She saw what it must have been like to be a widow bringing up a son in a village not her own. She saw it so clearly that she was astounded. It was as if she had an extra vision, as if the air itself brought the past with all its details nearer. The number of times the thin woman had been ill and people had said that she was weak and useless. She looked down at the thin woman's arm. It was so shrivelled, and dry.

Crichton Smith reveals years of back story, which immediately makes us feel sympathy for the character. We learn that she was stoic (strong) despite facing hardships with no support; that she made huge sacrifices for her son and that the difficulties she endured have taken their toll. We also see the 'fat woman' differently as she appears to care; we are also introduced to the theme of the sacrificing of one's own comforts for the sake of others.

If Crichton Smith had explained the back story of each character in full it would have taken up too much room and been quite boring.

Task 9

Look at the story *The Telegram* again.
1. How is each of the characters introduced to us?
2. What motivates of each of the characters (what drives them)?
3. How do the characters differ?
4. What do we learn about the background of the two women?
5. Crichton Smith created two very different characters in the two women. What do you think he hoped to achieve by this?

Stuck for ideas?

Good writers are always on the lookout for good characters. Inspiration can come from anywhere so try to be more aware of the people around you and learn to be a people watcher!

Some ideas of places you could find characters

- In a **good story**. If you find a good story, try to consider the motives of the people involved and the lives of these potential characters. What led them to this point in their lives?

- From **news reports**, either from a newspaper or on the internet.

- Characters from a **fairy tale** or **child's story**. Perhaps give them a new lease of life by putting them in a different story with different characters in a different time. A modern fairy tale is a common task in creative writing, but it also makes a great character exercise.

- On the **bus**, on the **street**, in a **shop**, **restaurant** or cinema. Basically **anywhere!** The key is to record them (discreetly) – see below for the next step.

Note: **Observing** people (in a subtle way) will give you plenty of material for the creation of your own characters. You should, from this point onwards, **keep notes** of your observations to create your three-dimensional **vibrant characters**. Use the following headings to help you. You can't observe people for too long – this is where you have to blend the **reality** with your **imagination** and make it up!

Physical description of the character you observed.

Slight, short, pale, with a shock of red curly hair.

Any actions that you want to record, for example, the way the character interacted with others; if they seemed confident or withdrawn; sad or happy.

Some attract people and are warm – others have the opposite effect. Write down details of all the minute actions that make them who they are.

Confidently shouting at her mother showing a complete disregard or respect for her elders.

Can you make up a back story about them? What brought them to this place today? Keep it brief.

The girl, fed up with having her future dictated by her elders, has taken matters into her own hands and is arranging her own marriage.

She contrasts very well with her large brutish father and her very traditional and demure mother. Her two little brothers also create a nice contrast. Plenty of scope for conflict.

Non-human characters

If you include non-human characters in your story, you will deal with the **abstract** and **personification.**

Some wonderfully engaging short stories have been written from the point of view of characters that are non-human. The genius is that they have moral or physical dilemmas just like a human character.

A great example of a novel that uses anthropomorphism (in which human traits and emotions are given to non-human characters) is *Watership Down* by Richard Adams, which is told from the perspective of a group of rabbits. *The Ship Who Sang* by Anne McCaffrey is a science fiction series written from the perspective of an intelligent spaceship.

If you try this approach, don't rely solely on the ending (such as a big reveal that the characters you've been describing aren't human) – the rest must be strong too. Have a **strong theme** – try to include an element of human condition, such as suffering or jealousy. **Make your non-human characters as human as possible.**

Task 10

1. List as many objects or animals that could be a potential character for a story. Pick one and write a paragraph on the character's dilemma, situation (or back story) and what the theme of the story could be as your character should still represent some element of what it is to be human. Some interesting ideas have been suggested for you below but try to think of your own.

Anything other-worldly such as mermaids, werewolves and other fantasy figures; everyday objects (perhaps something that has been discarded and no longer needed); pieces in a game such as chess; animals, illnesses or **abstract** feelings such as jealousy. With all of the above you should remember to develop the characters, keep them believable and maintain the characterisation until the end.

2. Over to you! Copy and complete the following table. Do this as many times as you need to.

Your strongest character idea.	Description of the character. For example: appearance, actions, personality. Any brief back story notes.	Identification of any flaws or weaknesses.	Ideas of setting and plot for the character. Any characters that would create a contrast? Any themes that would work well for this character?

Remember: the most lovable characters are flawed. 'To err is human...' (Alexander Pope). Reveal their little issues, big issues, less than perfect character traits or hang-ups. That's what makes them make them real and often drives the story forward.

The passion killer – avoid passive storytelling

'Don't tell me the moon is shining. Show me the glint of light on broken glass.'

Anton Chekhov

Sometimes, even although you have both planned and developed a fantastic story (and remembered to use language for effect) your writing can still feel quite dull. You may have been told by your teacher to 'show not tell'.

The problem could be that you feel that everything has to be explained in order for the story to make sense, so you rely on exposition (information necessary to move the story forward). This style of writing will kill your story. First, try to determine whether you actually need to fill in the gap and then see if you can you do it through revealing actions or reactions.

Look at the example below.

> Sharon, Elizabeth, Alexandra and Lisa were afraid as they entered an old, unlikely shop in a tiny village. It looked as if it hadn't been open in years. There were old shelves with a sparce eclectic range of random items. No prices were displayed yet the shopkeeper seemed to know the price of them all, right down to the last penny. Even the dogs (Dolly and Alfie) appeared uneasy.

A better version using actions and senses may look something like the example below.

> Sharon, Elizabeth, Alexandra and Lisa exchanged uneasy glances as the door creaked open unwillingly. A light sprinkling of dust fell from the heavy rusty door hinges and a tiny ominous bell alerted the owner of the shop to their presence. Upon the heavy, wooden shelves, random unrelated items sat unapologetically side by side. Lisa stepped forward hesitantly reaching for a small, white candle perched precariously on the side of the nearest display. 'Seven pounds and nine pence', bellowed the voice behind the counter without so much as looking up. Dolly growled a warning and Alfie whimpered as they turned and fled back into the safety of daylight.

Do you see how it is a little more detailed? Statements such as 'they were afraid' have been shown (described more fully) through slightly more detailed descriptions or actions – 'they exchange glances' suggests an unease clearly enough to the reader. There is some telling (Lisa stepped forward) but it is balanced by the action of the shopkeeper bellowing out the price and the dogs fleeing in fear. Improvement in this area of your writing is more about being aware that there are ways of showing actions or feelings that are more descriptive and varied. Like all aspects of writing it will improve the more you try.

Although this can seem complicated at first, it is well worth trying to understand. The following section highlights the problem of writing in a **passive** voice and explains why you should avoid doing so.

Look at the example below.

The horse was groomed by Janice.

In this case, the subject of the sentence ('the horse') does not perform any action. The object that is acted upon has become the subject of the sentence. **Passive means lifeless.** This sentence is lifeless. However, if we subtly change the above to:

Janice groomed the horse.

'Janice' is now the subject of the sentence. This tiny change has meant that the sentence is now written in the active voice and the **phrase feels more natural and lively**. Active means lively. On the whole, using a **passive voice is a less concise** way of writing and your sentences will end up being much more wordy. It is especially important, when you are developing character, to **try and avoid a passive style of writing** – it distances the reader and **stops the audience from engaging!**

Task 11

Try to change these passive sentences to reflect an active voice. Don't worry if you struggle with this at first – it will become easier. See the back of the book for suggested answers.

- The forest was planted by Albert.
- This ring was given to me by my sister Orla.
- The drinks were poured by Autumn.
- The bricks that broke the windows were thrown by Calum and Leon.
- The race was won by Iona.

Remember: Try to avoid simple sentences and instead of simply 'telling' the reader that something happened; *'The bricks that broke the window were thrown by Calum and Leon'* try to explain the action through description. *'Calum and Leon picked up the cold, hard lumps of stone and hurled them in the direction of the large window: a shattering noise broke the silence'.*

Can you see how the sentence feels more lively now? Sometimes a simple sentence just needs a **little expansion, or further description,** to improve it.

Further examples:

Annalise was a tidy girl.

Again, this simple clause is boring. Think about how you could **show** that she was tidy.

At the end of the day, Annalise carefully folded away all of her clothes and placed them neatly in her top drawer.

The garden was hot.

Here you could add in description of the effect of the intense heat, such as:

The flowers were wilting, the earth was baked dry and the cat was lazily searching for a small spot of shade.

Task 12

Your turn: Improve the following paragraphs by adding more description. The first sentence has been started for you. Your revised paragraph will be longer depending on how much description you add.

The classroom was chaotic and Lizzie was finding the work stressful. The new textbook was challenging and she was falling behind with her homework which was making her feel quite unwell. Her mother was trying to help, but it had been a long time since she had attempted this type of work and she was struggling to understand herself.

The commotion from the disengaged pupils could be heard from the other end of the long corridor. A peek into room 016 revealed a small group of girls with far more urgent issues to discuss than the themes in 'The Great Gatsby'. Behind them, Jake Maloney (who was having his third meltdown of the day) protested wildly at the outrageous injustice of his imminent removal from 'the situation' he and he alone, had created….

Remember to edit each sentence carefully and try to write with an active voice (look for overuse of the words **'was' and 'were'**, which may indicate passive voice). Always try to **show** how the scene looks, or how the action unfolded, rather than simply telling. Consider the **five senses** when writing character reactions. Never in real life do captions pop up and explain to other people what is happening – the written word is not so different. If you cut out exposition your writing will instantly improve. Be creative: find another way. Finally, if there is something you do need to explain, don't worry, just be skilful and try to keep it to a minimum.

Setting

Setting refers to all of the details of location and time of our story. This is a much more important aspect of storytelling than many pupils realise, and it must be considered at the planning stage. It should never be an afterthought or introduced at the start of your story then forgotten.

Setting usually refers to:

1. **The time** the story is set, for example: a period of history; present day or a point in the future. This could also include events from history such as a story set during the COVID-19 pandemic or the Second World War.

2. **The place** in which the story is set, such as the main location or immediate surroundings. These could include a specific country, city, town, village, street, house, room, car, stable, bus. The list is endless.

When you are reading (or watching) texts, it is important to consider the time and place in which the story was written because as well as giving it **context**, which helps us understand the story, it may reflect the experiences and views of the writer. Iain Crichton Smith grew up in small and remote village and many of his stories comment on the attitudes of the small communities of that time and place. *The Telegram* is set in a small village where everybody knows everybody's business. This creates conflict between one of the women in the story who is considered an outsider in the community despite having lived there for many years. It also reinforces the theme of the devastating effects of war. *The community didn't even understand what the war had to do with them nor why their sons had to be involved.*

Setting can be an excellent way to create conflict and interest if you create contrasting settings for your characters. For example, if they are removed from their normal environment / comfort zone, they may feel uncomfortable; they may question the lives and values of others; they may struggle to fit in / learn something important about themselves.

Task 13

Choose a character who is at odds with their surroundings (put them in an unlikely setting). Read through the examples in the table below to help you. Try to create some interesting ideas that you could use in your own stories.

Examples:

Character	Setting	Potential conflicts (consider values, think of the little details that may be an issue and the bigger things too. These could be humorous or serious.)
A prehistoric teenager from caveman times	A modern-day setting	• Hunting down fellow pupils' pets to eat. • Equality in society instead of very set gender roles. • Activities that don't centre around the family.
A ghost child	A school setting	• Not having a family home like other children to do homework in and constantly getting in trouble for it. • Feeling different and being unable to fit in. • Feeling exasperated with the kind of petty dramas that mortal human beings involve themselves with.

Now that you have some ideas for setting, remember to describe them in detail. A very detailed description will help engage the reader. You must keep the description going for as long as you can. Look at the following passage and take note of all of the tiny details. Underline (or copy into your jotter) all of the examples of setting and try to identify the techniques used, for example: metaphor, word choice or alliteration.

'...the boys passed between the barn and the row of chicken houses, their feet stirring up the carpet of brown feathers dropped by the moulting chickens. They paused before going down the slope to the lake. A fluky morning wind ran among the shocks of wheat that covered the slope. It sent a shimmer northward across the lake, gently moving the rushes that formed an island in the centre. Kildeer, their white markings flashing, skimmed the water, crying their shrill, sweet cry. And there at the south end of the lake were four wild ducks, swimming out from the willows in open water.'

The Stone Boy by Gina Berriault

Use the following table format to help you.

Example of setting	Techniques used such as: metaphor, word choice, alliteration.

A change in setting can indicate a change in tone or to appear symbolic of or foreshadow something that will happen later on in the story (like a clue).

In summary

- **Plan** in your setting in detail, which should include time and place. It must never be an afterthought as it is a valuable tool to help you highlight the key ideas of your stories.
- **Consider** how the setting fits in with your characters and supports any themes.
- **Keep the setting going** all the way though.
- Use lots of imagery and **detailed description** to bring your setting to life. You can **evoke a really wonderful atmosphere** through detailed description of setting.

Plot and narrative

Pupils often mix up plot and narrative and it is important to know the difference.

The plot is the main event in the story-your initial idea.

The narrative is the way you make those events unfold and will include the narrator's perspective or emotions.

One simple storyline can be crafted into a very impactful, and original, final piece of imaginative writing through a careful and considered use of narrative structure and style. So, even if you can't think of an amazing storyline, you can still gain good marks.

Plot lines

Create a bank of plot lines (story ideas). You should already have made a start on this from the work you did on 'character and theme'. Try to write your own list of 5-6 ideas. Pick the best and add development notes on characterisation, themes, genre, setting, structure or anything else you want. Be as detailed as you can. If it isn't working out – choose another. Below are a few ideas to help you if you are stuck. The first example has been fleshed out for you to show how you could start to develop a plot line from a simple idea. It isn't finished: you would have to continue to fill in the details, but the bones are there.

Plot ideas	An example of the plot developed into a more detailed idea	Initial development notes	Structure	Themes	Setting	Genre
Tell the story of an injury, either psychological or physical.	A young boy living on the streets in 19th Century Edinburgh. Has a deep fear that is holding him back and putting him in further danger.	He is frustrated and fearful – presents as angry. Lonely, distances himself from others. He is misunderstood and sad. He feels guilty and hides his past. He struggles with trust. He lives in fear and danger.	Structure – the psychological injury is revealed at the end through a formal, short news report revealing him as the victim. This will appear shocking to the reader and evoke empathy for the protagonist (hero).	Isolation, not fitting in betrayal, social anxieties.	19th Century Edinburgh. Old Town. Setting to depict street life in one of Edinburgh's back streets. Research 'Fleshmarket Close' and 'Sugarhouse Close' for examples.	Crime, realism, historical fiction loosely based around life in the dark and scary streets of 19th Century Edinburgh.

Plot ideas	An example of the plot developed into a more detailed idea	Initial development notes	Structure	Themes	Setting	Genre
A school pupil struggles to make friends. They have an unexpected visit from a great, great grandmother. How does she help?		Continue...	Continue...	Continue...	Continue...	Continue...
Seven characters each take on a personality influenced by the colours of the rainbow.						
Bored in her bed all day, a sick child entertains herself by writing stories about people, but the people are real and experience everything she writes.						

Tip

With such a restriction on word count you may want to keep the timeframe short – a moment, an hour, an afternoon, a day or a week (rather than years). If you are really confident with **time hopping**, then you could try a longer period of time or use flashback (see below).

The development stage – bringing your storyline to life

You are now at the point where you have to decide on the best narrative structure and style to enhance your story. Read through the following before you start planning.

Each story has a structure to show that events in the plot that relate to each other. We sometimes call this cause and effect.

Linear narration – all in order!

A popular choice by pupils: written in chronological order (as the story would naturally unfold in real life) and often narrated in past or present tense. Your story line must be very strong to pull this off as there is little creativity involved in the structure. If you do choose to use a linear narration, do be careful not to fall into passive story telling style (see page 31). Typically, the stages are:

- *The set up stage*: you introduce characters, setting and a normal situation or 'equilibrium'. Try to start with a hook – 'Orla was a child from a different time'.

- *The disruption*: you present an incident or a motive, such as a decision by a character. This changes the course of a story for you and sets you up for the next stage.

- *Rising action*: this is where you develop the story conflict. Give your character a problem or introduce complications. Think about your chosen themes, for example: if you had picked 'Man vs nature' it could be that your character faces several dangerous situations while on a journey. The story isn't really about the journey at all, it is about the strength he has to overcome the obstacles in his way such as: snow, bitter cold, driving rain or hunger. It is about his determination against all odds to survive. Throw everything you can at your characters to prevent them from reaching their goal.

- **Climax or turning point**: this stage is where you reach a high point of tension, the character may face his biggest fear at this point. It allows you to turn your story towards the finishing post.

- **Falling action and final resolution**: these are the final stages of your story – and the last chance to impress your examiner. You can leave the story open-ended, perhaps with some unanswered questions – this would engage the reader as they wonder what happens next. Or you could, in the case of a suspense story, have crafted an unexpected twist or two.

No 'once upon a time' required

Remember that you are limited in a short story in the sense that you have a word count in most school-related writing. You run the risk of allowing yourself too much exposition (explanation) which as we know can kill the pace and your audience engagement.

To avoid this common pitfall, you could miss out the set-up phase and launch straight into the action. This is a great technique for several reasons. Firstly, it is easy to do – the readers are engaged because they have been launched straight into rising action as you throw problem after problem at them. Secondly, you will have also provided an enigma (see below). If you struggle to create engaging openings try this method.

Example

In the story *Goldilocks and the Three Bears,* you would perhaps have started something along the lines of: 'Goldilocks stared straight into the eyes of a family of bears as she sat alone at the kitchen table.' Although you don't have to remember this term, this device is sometimes known as the 'Fichtean Curve': a focus on rising action, climax and then falling action only. You can still reveal character, theme and setting through the rising action. It requires some planning and thought of course, but it is an excellent choice.

Non-linear narration – out of order!

This is the equivalent of story time travel. You will use time-altering devices such as flashback deliberately **for a chosen effect** (which you can justify if asked!). When used effectively, a flashback is a great device for a short story as it can help you: *add suspense and build tension; hint at a theme you are going to explore; reveal a time that haunted a character (or which had a major impact); help you to 'time-leap' effectively; reveal a character memory which relates to or introduces the main story.* Do make sure you know when the story needs a flashback and be sure to use the correct tense. You may want the flashback to be in the past tense but then change to the present tense for the continuation of the story. Try to keep your flashback brief.

Example

A perfect and oft used, but subtle, example of an effective flashback is this one from *The Great Gatsby* by Scott Fitzgerald: *'In my younger and more vulnerable years my father gave me some advice that I've been turning over in my mind ever since. 'Whenever you feel like criticizing anyone,' he told me, 'just remember that all the people in this world haven't had the advantages that you've had.'*

Any changes that you make to the natural timeline will result in a non-linear timeline. You could start with the end and then let the story unfold.

Parallel story structures are a more complex way of non-linear story telling. An example is *Romeo and Juliet*. It is a love story between two people but it is interwoven with the conflict between the Capulets and Montagues. The two different plot lines become interwoven – joined by theme. Why do this? *To add more complexity to your story; to add background; to reveal an incredible ending, when the two stories combine, or to reinforce theme or character backstory*. Be sure to plot each story on a timeline first before you try to interlink them. You can also tell one simple story from the perspective of two different characters -perhaps by telling the story in one half of your essay then starting the same story again. Told from a different character's perspectives the audience will have a first-person narration from two different viewpoints. This could produce some very interesting conflicts and could be as complex or simple as you like, however never overcomplicate for the sake of it.

Circular structure is a lovely way to return to the beginning of the story, at the end. The trick here is to make sure that your characters have undergone a transformation, even although the beginning and ending of the story are the same. The child's story, *If you Give a Mouse a Cookie* by Laura Joffe Numeroff, is a perfect example of a circular story structure. It illustrates cause and effect very simply as the narrator shows all the things that the mouse will want to do if you give him a cookie. Which of course ends with him needing another cookie.

Other examples of non-linear structures are where a writer has used **stream of consciousness or dramatic monologue** style of narration – see the next chapter.

Other useful narrative techniques

Opposites attract. You have already learned that conflict drives plot and keeps the audience interested. Try to build in as many contrasts as you can, for example characters who are very different in appearance and outlook (the two women in *The Telegram* would be a great example); characters who are in conflict with, or out of place in, their surroundings; characters who are acting in a way that does not reflect or align with their true values. We sometimes call these structures 'binary oppositions'. They will be in most stories you have read or films you have watched. Can you list some now?

Use enigmas or little mysteries to keep your audience guessing about the story, make sure you use enigmas from start to finish. You could: start in the middle of the action without explanation; start with a concise flashback statement; withhold some information; jump (carefully) to a different plot point. You may have a very enigmatic character who appears complex and mysterious.

> **Tip**
>
> *Learning to use narrative devices properly is an opportunity to be original and creative and will make a big difference to the quality of your work. Do make sure that events are in an* <u>order which makes sense to your reader</u>*.*

Task 14: Planning

Take one of the plotlines that you created at the start of this chapter. Using sticky notes, write each of the key points of the story on one of your notes. Now try moving them around to see which structure works best and feels the most engaging. Once you are happy, try to see where you can add conflict and enigmas (see above).

For further information on narrative structure consider researching:

*   The Hero's Journey
*   Fichtean Curve
*   Circular narrative structures
*   Frame narratives
*   The three act structure

Language – a reminder!

Undoubtedly the best way of learning to use language is to study how others have used various techniques to create meaning, evoke atmosphere or even shock the reader.

For the purpose of the English curriculum, when we refer to language, we are generally referring to: effective word choice, original imagery, varied sentence structure and punctuation for effect. The worksheet below offers a reminder of how to improve your use of the techniques listed. Do experiment lots to see what works for you.

Technique	Tips
Word choice	Always look for the most **effective vocabulary** to use. Revise the work you will have done on **connotation and denotation**. There are always different 'shades of meaning' depending on the connotation you want to evoke. Look for **other synonyms** to see if there is a stronger or a more unusual or **emotive choice**. Do not feel the need to use 'big words' for the sake of it (especially if you are not completely sure if they make sense in the context of your sentences). Aim for a **sophisticated** and **confident expression** and above all be sure that the word you choose is exactly the one you need.
Imagery	It is a real skill to be able to substitute an explanation with a **powerful image** to better **help the reader visualise** what is happening in your story. **Metaphors; similes** and **personification** for example, are all techniques that you can use to help you **communicate brilliantly** (research if you have forgotten). In the short story *The Telegram*, (see pages 14–18), Iain Crichton Smith refers to the document (the telegram itself) as a 'missile' and then goes on to explain that it is 'aimed at them from abroad'. A missile is a deadly weapon, and this document delivered the news of death which brought utter devastation upon the target family: it was to be feared as a weapon would be. Your imagery should be **well thought out**, **powerful** and **original**. Remember that an **image is worth a thousand words**. **Revise imagery techniques now if you need to.**

Technique	Tips
Sound techniques	By using both visual and **auditory images** you will **evoke a stronger reaction** from your audience as they imagine through their senses – include the **sense of sound**. A beautiful example is in the poem: *To Autumn* by John Keats, as he brings the landscape to life through imagined sounds: *'And full-grown lambs loud bleat from hilly bourn;* *Hedge-crickets sing; and now with treble soft* *The red-breast whistles from a garden-croft;* *And gathering swallows twitter in the skies.'*
Punctuation and varied sentence structure.	It is taken for granted that at 4th level you will be able to use punctuation for the purpose of **creating concise meaning** (basic punctuation). You must now show your increasing skill by using all types of punctuation to create a **variety of sentence structures** for a considered effect. Consider: **short emphatic minor sentences**; climactic or **anti-climactic sentences**; deliberate repetition; effectively use **semi-colons** and or dashes and colons to create longer more complex sentences; brush up on the use of parenthesis; try a **question and answer** structure go bold with a **one sentence paragraph**s. There are publications that go into this in great depth and a solid grasp of language will serve you well as you work your way through the 4th level and senior phase English courses (and beyond).

Task 15

Now look at the short story *The Telegram* on pages 14–18 and find strong examples of the above. Remember to explain both how each technique has been used and why it is effective. Get into the habit of doing this each time you read a new text.

Accuracy is key

In addition to the above it is very important that your writing is technically accurate. You will be assessed on the standard of your literacy (both in English and other subjects across the curriculum). This means that the grammar must be correct and the spelling accurate. The sentences must be clear and concise and common errors, such as accidental repetition, removed before the final draft. This part of your writing must not be rushed. It is easier to correct as you progress and then again at the end. In short, you could fail an assessment if you neglect this part of the process – even if everything else is effective.

A great many pupils struggle with literacy. This does **not** mean that you can't succeed. There are a number of strategies you can use to help yourself. Everybody needs to edit their work – this is a job for you NOT your teacher. Below are some strategies that may help.

Make use of ICT to edit for errors	Try to **work with a sans serif font** (one that does not have little strokes at the end of the lettering, such as arial or comic sans) at a **size which is comfortable** for you and use a **coloured background:** pale green, peach and blue can be really effective. Work through **one small paragraph at a time**. Obvious errors in your text will be indicated with a red or blue underline and a right click of the mouse will offer an alternative. **Check** that you have selected the correct meaning. (right click 'synonym' for similar words).
Read out loud	There is research to show that this very effective strategy works. **Hearing ourselves read engages the auditory network** which allows us to identify errors **far more easily**. If you try to edit your work silently, the chances are you will miss a number of errors.
Ask for help	**Ask a friend** to read over your work. **Talk to your teachers**: there are a number of excellent strategies that can be employed to help you.
Learn the spelling rules	An internet search will very quickly equip you with a number of **spelling rules**. Learning them is relatively simple and will really speed up the editing process for you.

Bringing it all together

If you have completed all the exercises so far, you should now have the tools to plan, create, develop, evaluate and re-draft your piece of imaginative writing. You should aim to write between 850 and 1300 words.

Remember, the word count is only there to ensure you have enough space to demonstrate your writing skills: do stick to the word count for practice but do not fall into the trap of counting words and finishing when you reach your intended word count. Better to get as close you can and then on second draft, you can consider how you can cut it down to within the limit.

Planning tools

There is no right or wrong way to plan but never miss out this important stage. The purpose of a plan is to record all of the main points you want to use and to create a structure that is going to be most impactful. Remember that it is much easier to change the order of events in the story at planning stage rather than waiting until you have finished the first draft. Don't try to write from memory (otherwise known as 'winging it') as your lack of preparation will be evident. You will often be graded on your level of preparation. Quite simply, the planning stage is a significant part of the writing process and the more detailed the plan: the better the final piece. Try one or more of the methods below and use what works for you.

Mind map – a visual tool to lay out the order and detail of the story. Helps you keep track of the key points during the planning stage.

Sticky notes – can be used in combination with a mind map. The great thing about them is that you can write the key points of the story and play about with them until you have the order (or structure) that you feel works best.

A timeline – again, this works well with a detailed set of notes or a mind map.

You can also use the development notes you completed in the Plot and Narrative section!

Below is a checklist of the preparations you need to make before you write your draft.

Organise and revise the notes or work that you have done so far on: plot theme character setting narrative structure other narrative techniques	

Create a **detailed plan** bringing together your ideas (see above if you don't know how). You could also **use the development notes** you made in the plot and narrative chapter. You should now check your plan against the assessment criteria given to you by your teacher (or use the one below). Assessors need to measure your progress against key outcomes, as you may have to complete a self-assessment task. Do not miss out this important crosschecking stage – it will save you time later on.	
Start to **write your first draft** – take your time, work somewhere without distractions and take regular breaks. Don't worry if it takes you a few sessions to write your first draft – you have your plan to remind you.	
When you have completed your first draft, complete a **close technical edit** (see above) and work through the assessment sheet below. Try to **identify some targets** for your teacher (or yourself) in the form of a comment at the end of your first draft.	
You will **review the piece** again taking account of any teacher or peer comments and your own observations. A second draft may involve a complete restructure rather than just a 'correction'. Don't be disheartened if this is the case, no piece of good writing was ever a first attempt. Your re-drafts will be much easier and are part of the process. Remember to be realistic about the amount of effort required to produce an effective piece of writing at this level and beyond.	

The planning and assessment sheet below is a revision of all you have learned in this book. Use it during the planning stage to ensure all the essential elements of imaginative writing have been considered and developed.

After you have completed the first draft, you can use it as an audit sheet to double check where in your story you have explored each element and to what extent. This will help you identify targets for improvement. It is very thorough, but it will help you as you learn to be a brilliant writer!

Finally, before handing in to your teacher, write some notes on what you think worked well and why and which improvements you intend to take. For example, what may you need to develop, remove, or change and why.

Remember you are aiming for progress not perfection.

Assessment tool for 4th level imaginative writing

I have considered the genre of my piece of writing.	The genre of my writing is:	What typical genre conventions have I included?
The plot is believable and original?	Explain your plot line in one or two sentences.	What was the inspiration for your story?
Did you explore one (or more) themes?	What are the themes in your story?	How are the themes developed?
Have you fully developed your characterisation?	Who are your key characters? Do we learn of their backstory and key drivers or motivations? Have you described all aspects of their character? Are they flawed? How?	Where have you built in conflict for your characters?
Where and when have you chosen to set your story?	What details have made the setting really effective?	Was there any conflict or important links between setting and character?
Have you tried to use a specific narrative structure for effect?	Describe the narrative structure you have used and explain the effect you wanted to create.	Which other narrative techniques have you used?
Narration – from which point of view have you told the story?	What was the advantage of choosing to write from that particular point of view?	What worked well? What did you find challenging?
Have you used language effectively (and consistently) to try and engage the reader?	Give examples of language you have planned to include.	Which aspects of language could you have used to better effect? (Do this after you have finished your first draft.)
Did you check and edit your work thoroughly after handing in?		

Personal reflective writing

To reflect is to: analyse, consider and re-consider situations.

It is very probable that, during your time in an English classroom, you have been asked to write about a personal experience. As you reach 4th level and beyond, it is often expected that you will write reflectively, and this can be a challenging departure from an essay with a simple objective to simply recall an experience, such as a holiday or important event. You can still use the same topic for inspiration but writing reflectively requires a completely different skillset. This type of writing reveals an experience or moment that has perhaps taught you something; made you feel uncomfortable; changed your life or changed your point of view about something. The experience is often only a **catalyst** for reflection. You may wish to use a stream of consciousness style of writing.

What skills will I need? Although it is a form of non-fiction writing – you will still use many of the aspects of writing that you have learned in this book so far, such as **structure**, the **use of language** or the **exploration of theme**. You may still refer to **setting** in detail and you may replace the **characters** in your essay with yourself or discuss other people key to the experience that you are trying to tell. You may explore **conflict** within the story and you will most certainly be exploring a **theme**.

Try to create a bank of potential ideas for personal writing. In order to help you, start by listing all of the occasions that you have witnessed something that made you start to think differently about the world (or yourself) or taught you something you didn't know about yourself. Do this now.

What experiences are good to write about? Not all unfortunately! The choice of subject is crucial here. The following table should help you to sound out your idea and determine if it is worth developing.

Was the idea recent enough for you to remember and reflect upon?	I remember that day clearly. I was 18 months old.... (*X*)
	Last week, a seemingly insignificant event changed the way I saw the world... (✓)
Did the experience make you think about something differently? Did it teach you or reveal anything about yourself, others or the world you live in? Will it enlighten the readers about anything? Is it more than an account?	Explain –

Is it interesting, or thought provoking enough to you to spend a significant amount of time on?	
Did you observe something interesting and relatable that you want to document and comment on- perhaps a wider social issue?	Explain –
Did the experience help you grow as a person?	How...
Do you want to talk about a topic that your audience would also be able to relate to for example, what makes you happy?	Why? What is the topic.
Can you draw conclusions from the experience?	

Once you have decided on an experience you want to write about, you will have to analyse your thoughts and reflect upon them in detail. <u>In a really well written reflective essay, the reflection will outweigh the retelling of the story</u> – aim for this balance. The following tips should help you to write an effective piece of reflective writing.

- Through a deep dive into an experience of your choice, try to show an awareness of related wider social issues. Will your experience, once explored, add value to your readers? Many magazine articles are written in this style.
- You should try and draw at least one conclusion from your reflections. In other words, you should express what you have learned from the experience. This is best done throughout the entire piece of writing, rather than only stated within the conclusion.
- It does not have to be a life-changing experience: many great essays have explored small everyday occurrences that have led the writer to think deeply about something – or led them to question or confirm their values.
- Try to show real self-awareness – reflection should reveal something about the kind of person that you are (either explicitly or implicitly).
- You may wish to write in the style of 'first person' for this style of writing.
- Use reflective phrases throughout, such as 'looking back, this forced me to question my own beliefs', etc. Some more reflective phrases have been provided for you in the further ideas section.
- You may find yourself using a more informal style of language in this style of writing.
- You can create a lovely circle structure by returning to a beginning phrase, thought or title.
- Follow your heart and try to add real emotion.

Examples

There are many excellent examples of personal or personal reflective writing and the best way to learn is to read the work of others.

Example 1

E. B. White is best known for his famous children's books such as *Stuart Little* and *Charlotte's Web*. *Once more to the Lake* is a reflective piece he wrote about the long summers he spent with family. It is beautifully written. Look at the following extract.

> One summer, in about 1904, my father rented a camp on a lake in Maine and took us all there for the month of August. We all got ringworm from some kittens and had to rub Pond's Extract on our arms and legs night and morning, and my father rolled over in a canoe with all of his clothes on; but outside of that, the vacation was a success and from then on <u>none of us ever thought there was any place in the world like that lake in Maine</u>. We returned summer after summer – always on August 1st for one month. I have since become a salt-water man, but <u>sometimes in summer there are days when the restlessness of the tides and the fearful cold of the sea water and the incessant wind which blows across the afternoon and into the evening make me wish for the placidity of a lake in the woods</u>.

NOTE: The underlined parts of the extract show strong reflection or insight into the writer's memories. White uses the setting to reflect on his past. Note his use of beautifully embellished descriptions of setting just as you yourself may use in an imaginative piece of writing. It would be very easy for you to reflect on a memory of the past and at the same time embellish that memory with vivid imagery from a beautiful setting. **Try this** now.

Task 16

Your 'micro memory'

Write a vivid and detailed description of setting. Remember to use effective imagery, word choice and sentence structure.

The next extract is a completely different type of personal writing. Varaidzo explores issues around 'fitting in' and 'feeling different' as a young person – something many of us can relate to in one way or another. It is a **global** (largescale) **theme**. Refer back to the theme section of the book on pages 19–23.

Example 2

Read this reflection from a mixed-race writer who was the only child in her primary school in Bath who wasn't white. In *A Guide to Being Black*, Varaidzo discusses her experience of hearing the offensive 'N-Word' as the only black person in the room.

> At some point, the inevitable will happen. It will happen at a rave, or a club, or a party, where music is playing and people are dancing. A song will come on, usually a rap song, and amongst my generation it will nearly always be a song by Kanye West. This is when an elephant will sneak into the room, walking straight out of Kanye's mouth, dressed as a word that can't be spoken. They will notice at the same moment they notice me: the only black kid at the party.
>
> It's Kanye, so everybody knows the lyrics, and everybody is looking at me. I've got 30 seconds to a minute before the chorus hits to decide what to do. If I chant the word it will be public confirmation of my blackness, a deliberate display that says this word is mine and mine alone to say. That I am allowed. That is damn near a birth right. And in that moment of vindication it seems obvious that I'm going to sing along, because if rapping along to Kanye is one of the few privileges afforded to me as a black person, then of course I'm going to take it.
>
> Except, there are a few other things going on here. For a start, by being in the room, I am the only reason why the rest of the party can't say it. *I'm a big red stop sign in the middle of the dance floor*, a symbolic reminder of why they shouldn't use such a word and who they will offend. Without me there, the word is just another rhyme in a lyric. It's a tree falling in a forest conundrum: if a white kid raps all the lyrics to 'Gold Digger' and there isn't a black person around to hear it, is it still racist?

This writer uses an incident to address the problem of hearing the 'N-word' used in popular culture such as 'hip-hop' and American film culture (both for white and black kids). She explores the awkwardness experienced by all, in not knowing how to react for the best. As a result, her story leads on to the wider issue that we can all relate to. The piece is reflective throughout, explores a serious issue and yet is quite light-hearted in tone. The contrasting tone and subject matter is clever and lively to read. She draws a conclusion that there is no resolve other than 'to keep your fingers crossed for a radio edit' when you do hear it. It voices a very important issue in a, sometimes, humorous way.

Task 17

Now your turn. **Identify an important theme** and **write one paragraph** describing an experience related to that theme. Try to **use a contrasting tone.** An example would be the theme of the importance of friendships at school: the experience may have been a time you felt you were treated unfairly, or left out of something.

As we know, an idea alone does not guarantee a good essay. You have to develop your ideas just as you did for the short story writing. As this a personal reflective task, the assessor will expect to understand the impact the experience had on you and how you reflect or relate it to the wider world. Reflective phrases, such as *looking back*, *in hindsight* and *if I knew then…* do show some insight but you can do better by simply making insightful links to global themes.

Do the development task below for just one section of your strongest essay idea so far. It will form part of your plan. In the example above this could be the key memory of dancing with her friends to the inevitable Kanye West song. You would then do this for any other key points of the experience as they may have made you feel differently. You could also use a mind map if you prefer.

Task 18

The experience you are writing about:

Personal experience. How, at certain points, did the experience make you feel? Think about describing experience through the senses: sight, smell, taste, sound and touch. What emotions did it evoke? Can you describe the setting in detail?	
Reflection. Why was it a significant moment? How could it relate to others or a **wider social issue**?	

Once you have developed each key experience or memory of your essay, you are ready to decide on the structure of your essay.

How to structure an effective reflective essay

The following reflective essay structure is only one example for you to try once you have decided on the experience and wider issue you want to explore. You can use this if you are stuck but try to experiment with and consider other structures. The idea is to widen your experience of writing. You will get better the more you try. Aim to be original.

Introduction

You need an interesting and effective opening. Perhaps you could start in the thick of the action – remember to be descriptive. You should set the tone on your reflections. Introduce the event that is at the heart of your reflections.

Main body sections

- Continue to expand on each personal experience – use your development notes from Task 18 on page 51. Include facts and events in order but in a descriptive and engaging way. Remember sensory detail (use the senses and avoid a boring passive style of writing by showing action rather than telling every detail). Start to edit out details that aren't essential to the experience.

- Next, introduce the reflection. Remember, your job is to explain and explore an awareness of a wider social issue or human condition that relates to the experience you have chosen. Make sure this section feels authentic (genuine) and is well-planned. The goal here is to explore the significance of your experiences in an engaging way. How did they change you? What have your learned?

Conclusion

In your conclusion, make clear any change that has occurred as a result. Did it change your attitude to something or did it reinforce your values? Did it present an opportunity for a change of habits or actions? Did it highlight an awareness of a global theme? It is always a lovely touch to return in some way to the beginning of the essay – perhaps return to a key idea from the start of your essay, such as the title or an opening phrase. Be sure to leave your audience with a final thought. You can reflect into the future by thinking about how your experiences are going to affect your life from now on.

Your task will be to plan, create, develop, evaluate and re-draft a piece of reflective writing. You should aim to write between 850 and 1300 words – remember, word count is important but try to avoid counting every word. Get as close as you can, whilst including all the key points, and then fine tune upon second draft.

Planning and developing

You will create a detailed plan of your choice. (You could use a mind map, sticky notes or a simple timeline.) Use your development notes and the self-assessment sheet below to help you check and review your plan before you complete your first draft.

Assessment tool for 4th level personal reflective writing

Content Do you have an interesting and relevant story to tell?	What is the experience you are describing?	How does it relate to a wider issue?
Have you included enough reflection or are you re-telling too much of your story?	Is there clear and genuine reflection of the experience from a personal perspective? Are thoughts and feeling evident throughout? Have you revealed a sense of your personality? Does it reveal anxieties, errors of judgement, strengths (or weaknesses) or an important aspect of everyday life? Are you showing a high degree of self-awareness?	Have you reflected on a wider social issue? If so, what? Does the reflection feel genuine and insightful enough to engage your audience and elicit a response? Does the reflection outweigh the storytelling part or at least equal it?
Style Have you manipulated language for effect in order to engage your audience? Have you avoided unnecessary repetition or clichés?	Have you used plenty of reflective phrases? Is your language emotive where it needs to be? Did you remember to use plenty of imagery and to carefully consider your word choice? Is your title effective?	Sentence structure – have you been as creative as possible with your sentence types? Have you used punctuation for effect rather than just for basic functionality?
Have you tried to use a specific narrative structure for effect?	For example, did you start in the thick of action (such as a flashback) and then explore your ideas finally returning to some reference to the beginning? Did you use a different structure? Outline the structure.	What was the intention of your chosen structure? Did it work?
Did you check and edit your work before handing in?	What worked really well for this piece of writing?	What do you think your targets for improvement are?

When you have completed your first draft, carry out a close technical edit. Ensure you have identified some targets to work on for the second draft.

You may be asked to review the piece again, taking account of any teacher comments, peer comments and your own observations. Remember, a second draft may involve a complete restructure rather than just a few 'corrections'.

Learning to discuss, persuade and report

It is very likely, at this stage in your English education, that you will have to produce a piece of writing that asks you to either *discuss, persuade or report*. Your 4th level work is an ideal time to start building a portfolio of ideas so that you have several strong options ready for your senior phase writing portfolio.

A **report** is where you research aspects of a chosen topic and present the key information in a very structured, formal and factual style. It is helpful to set out your report in sections by using subheadings and remember to introduce and finish off your report in an interesting way.

By way of an example, if you chose to write about *the recent history of changes to the curriculum in Scotland,* you could organise your sections as follows.

- **Introduction** – for example: that the Scottish curriculum has undergone a number of changes in recent years.
- An outline and brief context of **the current curriculum structure** including the values that underpin it.
- **Broad General Education** – what it is and the ethos it encapsulates.
- **Senior Phase** – the exam led phase – the challenges and merits.
- **Previous curriculum changes** and why it was felt they needed improvement.
- **The benefits and challenges** that the new curriculum brought to pupils and teachers.
- **A brief comparison** between the effectiveness of the Scottish curriculum and leading education systems in other parts of the world.
- **The future of the Scottish Education.**
- **A conclusion** to summarise the key points above. You can still draw a conclusion in a report although it is most likely to be at the end.
- **A reference section**.

This is a very straightforward piece of writing and as long as you plan and research effectively you shouldn't have any problems. There is an endless number of topic choices. The tone will be neutral and factual. It is more likely that you may be asked to produce a more complex piece of writing at this stage.

Discursive and persuasive writing

Both of these styles of writing provide opportunities to demonstrate your writing skills – although the 'persuasive form' is the livelier of the two and is the main focus for the rest of this chapter. **In discursive writing** you tend to **argue both sides of a topic**. You show **merits and problematic issues** and both sides tend to be **relatively equally weighted** to show a **considered and balanced** approach. This is perfectly acceptable, but you do have to work a little harder to bring this style of writing to life.

In a **persuasive essay** you do **not need to present a balanced argument**. When we talk about argument in English, we really mean a **discussion**. This opens up a whole range of interesting topics so as well as current affairs type topics, you could pick a cultural topic or even **rant** (in a structured way) about something much more light-hearted that you think matters. If executed carefully you can **use humour, rhetoric and anecdotal evidence** to produce a **convincing and lively** piece. As with other types of writing, it is best to learn from reading as many good examples as you can. You must get a feel for what a **strong persuasive tone** is and how the language techniques can **create persuasion**. You will gain insight into as the effects of language and you will get ideas for potential topics of your own.

Where could I find inspiration? Watch Ted talks, YouTube presentations, documentaries and other current affairs programmes. Listen to **podcasts and radio debates**. Watch the **news.** Research magazine writers (check broadsheet newsprint publications such as **The Sunday Times** or **The Guardian**). The SQA English National Five website also has some examples that should be easily accessible to you. Many **persuasive articles** are included in Past Papers, which are available on the SQA website. It is essential that you spend some time researching topics so that you are motivated by your choice. If you didn't enjoy working on it, it will be unlikely that your assessor will enjoy reading it.

Topic choice

Is writing a boring essay topic cruel for the assessors of English writing?

AVOID clichéd (overdone) topics – ask your teacher if you are unsure. Examples of topics to be careful of include:

- the ethics of keeping animals in zoos for the entertainment of humans
- the pros and cons of school uniforms
- the grave dangers of the representation of size zero models in the media
- the debate over the legalisation of cannabis.

All of these ideas have been done to death. What ground-breaking, original information are you going to add?

There are many topics that have been overdone. However, if you can find a fresh or controversial approach to the subject, then there is absolutely no reason why you couldn't try. **'The influence of cannabis on the Flower Power generation'** with an investigation into their attitudes towards the drug as being 'counterculture', may produce a really lively debate. If you look for current arguments surrounding these types of topics, it is absolutely possible to find a new and interesting approach. Do not, however, copy anyone else's work; rather, combine ideas and consider other angles. Be your own devil's advocate and ask yourself a few 'test' questions over the topic. For example: *'is dog fighting cruel?'* Yes of course it is. Please, go no further.

The two most important things that you have to remember are that the topic must be original and that your examiner must enjoy reading it. Your assessor will not reward you for sending them to sleep.

Newsprint – types of newspaper

As you are writing an article that could potentially appear in a magazine or newspaper, it is useful to have a little background knowledge on the main types of newspapers in circulation.

An article from the table of publications below would be similar to a persuasive or discursive essay. **A report** would be more functional – perhaps to cover an event or incident. If you were a paid writer, the type of writing you produce would very much depend on the type of publication you are writing for.

Broadsheet newspapers

Type of newspapers	Features	Examples
Broadsheets	Although now mostly smaller in size, they were traditionally large. Considered respectable. **Content** Typically deal with subject matters such as: international or national affairs; culture and art. **Tone** is more serious and is less reliant on opinion, more factual and less biased (more objective). **Style** – sophisticated writing style, longer pieces, can be formal, usually very well written. Less focus on pictures. Demographic or target audience would be predominantly educated individuals or professionals.	*The Times, The Independent* (online only) *The Guardian, The Herald, The Telegraph, The Financial Times*
Mid-market tabloids	**Content** balances serious broadsheet style reporting with articles aimed more at human interest. So somewhere between broadsheet and tabloid.	*The Daily Mail, The Daily Express*
Tabloids or Red Tops	**Content** is less serious and contains more human interest stories, scandal, sport and celebrity culture. **Tone** is sensationalist and light-hearted. Not as sophisticated in terms of sentence structure and vocabulary as the broadsheet papers. Typically, journalists use puns and screamer headlines to catch attention. Can be more biased, informal and rely on opinion. Heavily reliant on images. Has a target audience (or demographic) of lower middle- and working-classes.	*The Sun, The Daily Record, Daily Star, The Mirror, Morning Star*

The press in the UK is governed by the Independent Press Standards Organisation (IPSO), which governs the content of UK newspapers to ensure they meet strict guidelines such as privacy. That said, the tabloids can still 'spin a story' (write it with their own angle) to make it more appealing to their target audience.

Task 19

Find a story that has been reported both by a broadsheet and a tabloid newspaper. Identify examples of:

* language – use of quotes, vocabulary and sentence structure.
* Tone
* Headlines
* Pictures and anything else that you can identify. What are the differences? Which do you find more believable? Which do you prefer and why?

Purpose

Media content (films, television programmes, magazine or news content) tends to be owned by corporations and companies, so the main purpose is usually for **profit**. In order to get the reader to purchase the content, it has to be entertaining in some way.

Some content can **perform a public service** – including government publications on public health issues such as alcohol abuse or mental health. Or the content could be to **promote** something such as a film or an event.

Here is where it can become a little problematic as all content can be said to influence audience **behaviours and attitudes either intentionally or unintentionally**.

This is especially true of social media content (as it is easily accessible to a wide range of society) but it is true of all content. When you write your persuasive article you are influencing your audience. Did you want to change their opinion or behaviours and how are you going to do it? By presenting serious concerns to your audience? By being sensationalist or emotive? Or by offering a reasoned and balanced argument?

Task 20

Research your favourite magazine, film or other media content and find out who owns the company.
To illustrate the power of media content, try to research news stories that have influenced a large section of society. Consider the following questions:

* What newspaper (or other media platform) was responsible?
* What was the effect? Try to find out how people change their behaviours – for example, did they vote for a particular political party for fear that something bad would happen if they didn't?
* Try to print off the article and then highlight the emotive language used to see why it was so influential.

Learning how to research

Depending on the topic you choose, you may have to carry out some in-depth research. This could take the form of facts or statistics (figures). You will want to use evidence to substantiate your claims or simply for you to gain further knowledge of your topic. The quality of your research will directly impact the quality of the final piece of work.

1. **Clarify**

   Take a moment to work out **what it is that you are actually looking for** in your search. You can start without a computer and just use pen and paper to **jot down ideas.** Try to think of **questions surrounding your key** ideas that you may want to explore. Writing out your research ideas before you start will help you focus and will result in **better research results.** If you get stuck then pop onto the computer and search for **what issues surround your topic.**

2. **Search**

   There are lots of different ways you can research but most pupils in school often just pick a search engine such as Google. There is nothing wrong with this, especially if you do not have access to academic journals or a large library of books to choose from.

   Type in some keywords – see your plan. If you don't get the results you are looking for you can **alter the search terms** – look at your list of key words.

   Use quotation marks around key words to help the search engine be more specific.

   Often, pupils are put off as they can't find exactly what they are looking for. Keep an open mind and be prepared to adapt or adjust the focus of your research.

3. **Thoroughly investigate your results**

   Google uses something called an **algorithm to predict** and best match what it thinks you are looking for.

   Skilled researchers know that they may need to work through the results and not simply rely on the first page.

   Look for results from official sites rather than opinion or forum sites: they will be more reliable.

   ## TIP

   Right click on the title of a result that has appeared in your search and click 'open in new tab' if you want to keep the rest of the search list open.

   Look for the words 'ad' or 'sponsored' to weed out advertising which may be quite **biased.** This will not be a reliable source of information.

4. **Evaluate your information**

   Once you land on a site you may be able to scan for specific information using a search box. *Tip: use control F or Command F on a Mac to bring up a search box.* The following table may help you to revise your research skills and make the most out of your search.

Questions to ask yourself	Actions
Open site and skim read. Is it easy to understand and does it seem relevant?	If so, continue. If not delete and move on and progress to the next site on the list.
Is the information it is going to offer answers to your particular question? Remember to bring up a search box to help you.	If not, go back to your results – you may need to be more specific with the wording of your search.
Is the content recent enough?	If not, move on. Outdated information will not add credibility to your argument.
Does it look credible?	Check to see if there is an author (look at the 'about page'). Be careful. You need to know how to use the information in your own essay without running the risk of plagiarising the work of others.
Is it purely opinion or backed by evidence?	To help you work this out, consider the purpose of the article. Is it selling you something? Or is it littered with **affiliate links**? Is it too **biased**? Perhaps it is trying to influence your attitude in an unconvincing way. A more balanced article of evidence is a safer bet. If you have any doubts, move on to the next result.
Is there an agenda (for example a political slant) behind the article?	This is often hard to know and the representation of information in the media is complex. There may be a hidden agenda. Most news platforms are owned by companies that exist to make a profit. Take a moment to consider the purpose of the article or content you have chosen before you decide if you can rely upon its contents.

Always cross-reference your information. This means, check another source. Being media savvy will stand you in good stead. 'Fake news' is big business and you should not just accept everything you read as fact.

Always take more notes from your research than you need and cite everything you used to form your opinions. As you are taking notes, copy the site address (URL) of the article, the author (if you found one) and the date accessed. This will help you to accurately note your references.

TIP

Only take key points away from the article and put them in your own words (paraphrase) straight away. Clearly highlight any direct quotes. Be sure to read the next section on summarising and **plagiarism!**

Summarising, paraphrasing and referencing

Nobody will be expecting you to make up your own research. You will use the work of others to add weight and credibility to your own essay and you need to know how to do it. You will have identified the information you want to use as your chosen research points and do not want to run the risk of plagiarising. The following steps should help you.

1.	Skim read the article to ensure it is relevant to your work. Re-read it very carefully. Use a dictionary to look up any unfamiliar words as not knowing them could result in a misunderstanding.
2.	Identify (highlight if you can) any key ideas and make a note of them in your own words (where possible).
3.	Write up each summary from your notes keeping it brief and making sure it is relevant to the points you are trying to present, reinforce or oppose.
4.	Check back to the original to see if the summary is completely accurate and ensure that you have not listed phrases or copied any chunks of the original text.
5.	Always reference the original text.

Example

It was noted that of all the senior leaders in the armed forces, **fewer than 25%** were under **the age of 25**. Although it **can take time to climb the ranks** required to reach the senior rankings, it is **not the only route to progression**. Many **young graduates are also qualified** to step into such positions.

- Summary: most high-ranking personnel in the armed forces are over the age of 25.

- **Paraphrasing** means to translate in your own words. If there is a short piece of text you would like to paraphrase: make sure you understand the meaning; use a thesaurus if you need to find another way of phrasing the point; be sure it makes complete sense; and remember to reference the original source.

Example paragraph: Not even a quarter of the high-ranking positions in the armed forces were filled by young recruits. Whilst experience is clearly an advantage, it is not the only way to advance a career. University graduates may well have the valuable skills required to succeed in the type of jobs that require such important decision making (Mattinson, 2022).

- **In-text references** should be used when you have quoted directly, paraphrased or summarised because it tells the readers where you found the information that you are using. You need to use the author's last name and the year of publication. (Mattinson, 2022). If you use a direct quote use the page number and remember to use quotation marks: " …fewer than 25% were under the age of 25"(Mattinson, 2022, p.71).

- **In-text references with no author** can be cited with the first few words of the title and the date (*Equality in the Royal Navy,* 2022).

- For very long web addresses, break off at the first dash or hyphen.

- To cite an article in the reference section of your essay you need:

1. Author of the article.

2. Title on the page or of the section of the page you used in quotes.

3. Title of the web page, in italics, found in the address bar.

4. Name of the publisher of the page,

5. The date the page was published or last updated (day month year),

6. URL of the web page.

   For example: Jones, Alice. *"New toys."* Consumer Reports. Hearst Inc., 10 March 2015, http://consumerreports/newtoys.

References should be listed by surname in alphabetical order.

A bibliography is a list of all the work that you consulted rather than a reference list which includes only the sources you referenced. If you require a more detailed guide to referencing search 'Harvard Referencing' in a search engine.

Plagiarism

The Oxford English dictionary defines plagiarism as presenting someone else's work as your own without acknowledgement. This could be intentional but is more likely to be careless referencing or lazy paraphrasing or summarising. The consequences are severe. You can easily find an online plagiarism checker which will check your work for anybody else's references.

Manipulating statistics

One of the main reasons for researching for information is to find evidence from credible sources that back up your main ideas. However, the research you find may not always be as much in your favour as you hoped. You can sometimes manipulate the information to sound more supporting than it actually is. Which do you think sounds better: "24% of the population chose not to vote" or "nearly one quarter of the entire population chose not to vote"? Possibly the latter.

Task 21

Can you think of a different way to present the following information? The first one has been done for you.

Fewer than 25%	Not even one quarter
More than 50%	
2 out of every 8 people	
50 in every 100 cats	
Three quarters of all cars	

Creating structure through topic sentences and linkage

You will already be aware of the need to use topic sentences to create a sense of order and clarity within your essay. The use of topic sentences is non-negotiable (you have to use them) so get into the habit of writing them into your plan as soon as you have decided what key points you will explore in each section. Topic sentences make excellent planning tools. It is relatively easy to re-arrange your sections at the planning stage to create the most logical order before you start adding your evidence. Do make them specific enough that they provide an introduction to the central idea but not overly explanative that they give away too much.

A topic sentence:

- **Introduces** the key point, or points, of the paragraph, almost like a mini introduction. Note that although most topic sentences appear naturally at the start of the paragraph, you can also place them further on, for example at a point where you change your argument.

- Acts as **a transition** (or connection) back to the previous paragraph or point.

- **Provides a structure** to adhere to while writing the rest of the essay (almost like a plan).

- **Will make your writing stronger** and ensure your argument is in a logical order.

Linkage – different types of transition words or phrases

The following linking phrases, when included in your topic sentences, will help you to transition through your argument seamlessly (actually you can, and should, use them throughout your essay to build a well-structured argument). Do make sure you pick the correct ones though. For example, there is no point in you using the word 'however', which suggests a change in the direction of an argument, when you actually just wanted to add more supporting evidence. Similarly, do not use phrases such as 'in addition to', when you want to add in opposing point!

Function of your topic sentence	Notes	Suggested vocabulary
To **expand** on a point or **add ideas**.	The rest of the paragraph should present similar research, or evidence, which exemplifies or expands on the key points.	Firstly, secondly, thirdly, finally, furthermore, another, likewise, in addition to, additionally, similarly, also, moreover, this supports, exemplifies, as demonstrated by, can be seen as, for instance, such as, as an example, without doubt or unquestionably.
To **compare and contrast**.	The vocabulary in this topic sentence should reflect words that show differences or comparisons.	However, yet, on the other hand, conversely, although, on the contrary, in the same way that, that aside, despite this, notwithstanding, this aside, nevertheless.

Did you know that turning your topic sentence into a question also makes it easy for you to present contrasting evidence? |

Function of your topic sentence	Notes	Suggested vocabulary
To start a conclusion.	You will want to introduce vocabulary that suggests that you have drawn a conclusion and are about to close the argument.	In summary, in conclusion, for these reasons, in short, as a result, overall it may be said or in closing. You can also end on a 'call for action'. This works well because it involves your reader. You could make a prediction (which has been justified by your evidence); make a recommendation based on your research; or end on a question that asks the reader to make up their own mind or take action.

Example

The fashion industry is **unquestionably** *one of the biggest polluters worldwide.* *Fast fashion manufactures cheap clothing at a rapid speed which often ends up unworn and obsolete after a dangerously short period of time. Last year the fashion industry created (and emitted) more carbon dioxide than all airplane journeys and maritime transport combined. As recently as last year as much as 10% of all carbon dioxide polluting the earth came from the fashion industry (Earth.org 2022). 92 million tonnes of clothes waste was created and 20% of all wastewater produced came from dyeing and washing clothes (Earth.org 2022). These shocking statistics show the importance of the concept of sustainable fashion.* **(Holmes, 2022. The Lying the Which and the Wardobe)**

In the above example we can identify a simple structure which first **introduces** the argument that the fast fashion industry is a significant polluter then expands the idea by clarifying how this occurs (through the speed in which the clothing items are processed and then consequently discarded). Finally, Holmes exemplifies these statements with statistics showing the extent of harmful carbon dioxide emissions and finishes with a summary sentence.

Remember: **introduce, expand and exemplify.**

 Task 22

Look at the 'Sgt. Pepper's Lonely Hearts Club Band' article on page 71 and underline all of the topic sentences. Now underline the evidence in the remaining paragraph that expands the sentence.

Planning your essay

Carry out some initial google searches about your chosen topic and decide what the **main arguments or points of discussions are.** What are the issues surrounding your topic? **Look for new lines of thought or evidence to** keep your work current. Pick **4-5 key areas.** Do this <u>even if</u> you have prior knowledge of the topic already. These BIG ideas will form the individual sections of your essay. It is important in a persuasive essay to convey your stance (opinion). You will do this through tone. If you are angry, let it show.

Example

My chosen topic is **'the increasing popularity of home schooling'.** I am going to convince my audience that home schooling <u>is a good thing</u>.

I am going to use a simple visual mind map. Having done some initial research (1-2 hours), I have decided my key areas might be as follows.

1. <u>**The scale of the growing trend and why it has increased**</u>. This will act as a good introduction to the topic and I can use statistics (figures) to grab reader's attention. Research (BBC article, HMSC figures, .gov website on home sch)

2. <u>**Evidence to show that pupils learn better in a comfortable environment**</u> Research (Mental health for children UK/HSUK/psychology for education site). Home schooling – (lessons from home)

3. <u>**The idea that quality learning and teaching can be presented in a more natural context.**</u> Advantages of experiencing learning through everyday activities and the advantages this presents. Research (BBC article, HMSC figures,.gov website on home sch)

4. <u>**Riposte (a counter argument) addressing the concern that learners could miss out on social aspects of life – for example teamwork.**</u>

    Although this is counterproductive in terms of my strong argument FOR home schooling, it shows that I have addressed some of the potential problematic issues. Research (HSUK and BBC:22 article)

5. <u>**The availability of ICT – I will argue that for many, it is more possible than ever before to work from home and still in a collaborative way.**</u>

    This could mean that the traditional school model is now outdated. This gives me a really strong finish. I am making a bold and controversial statement but I have strong evidence to back this up. Research (increased sales of Tech equip. TechUk)

Additional notes on style, tone

I am going to build a positive and inquisitive tone backed by facts I have researched on the numbers of home schoolers increasing. I will use light-hearted humour and make it lively and engaging. I think I can still make some serious points. It will be chatty but persuasive.

Putting it all together – how to build a persuasive argument

The following will help you plan for an in-depth essay of around 1000-1300 words. Have a copy of the assessment criteria and your plan in front of you to refer to at each stage. This will save you time in the long run.

Step 1

Introduce the topic through a lively and concise introduction. Having an introduction in the plan will help you stay focused. Remember to make it engaging (see the persuasive techniques chapter for help). I am going to set the scene by remembering my home-schooling experience. I will try to use a climactic structure leading to a little reveal I am at home. This will engage the reader.

At some point in the introduction I must make clear the focus of my essay. If you need help with persuasive language ideas look at the following chapter.

> **Introduction** - It's 9.05. and in the corner of my 'desk' a pile of English books is waiting to be opened. Registration is complete we have been: informed of all of the extra curricula activities available this week; reminded for the hundredth time to return our subject choices to the guidance department (mine is still in the bottom of my bag); and been severely warned about the dire consequences of not handing in homework a week before the due date. Period 1 English with Miss Mattinson has just begun. My young sister is spilling Rice Crispies on my copy of Sailmaker. I try not to rise to the bait. I am sitting in the kitchen – welcome to home schooling, the new way to learn. This was a common scenario during the Covid-19 pandemic, but is it now a growing trend? I think so.

This last line makes clear my intent – to argue that home schooling is a growing trend. I like to avoid the statement 'In this essay I intend to' and make my writing more natural and chatty in tone. It is still formal enough but less 'mechanical'.

Do this now.

Step 2

You now simply need to work through each of the key areas in your plan. Introduce each area with a topic sentence and thoroughly develop it (by presenting and exploring your strongest research and by both expanding and discussing each area thoroughly before moving on to the next). Remember to use linkage and plenty of persuasive language techniques (see next chapter).

The aim is to build a considered, well-researched and solid argument. **Don't forget** to have at least one opposing idea and to ensure all of your key ideas are different – you don't want any overlap. Each section is almost a mini essay (although they must all link together to form your entire argument). To help you develop and expand your points, try to include:

- **Ideas which are along the same lines** as your key ideas (perhaps by a different writer or research study) and which will expand your argument (**develop your line of thought**). **Different ideas** that also back up your argument, to make your case stronger. **Key quotes** that exemplify or strengthen your point (used sparingly). **Opposing ideas** which you can acknowledge but perhaps offer some solution to – or dismiss, sensibly, having first acknowledged the idea. In your final essay you will use linking sentences and phrases in order to seamlessly build your argument.

Do you see how you are building a little case study for each section which will, when pieced together, create a strong convincing argument?

Remember – set all quotes out properly as shown on pages 60–61 and include the references in your bibliography.

Note that your key research points below can easily be made into topic sentences – you can expand the sections as needed. As a rule of thumb, you need at least half a page of evidence for each key point. You may not use it all in your final essay.

Repeat the process for each key idea. Keep the tone lively and interesting. Remember that the style is important. Experimenting with the use language such as word choice, imagery and sentence structure is key to improving your grade.

(Example – key idea as a topic sentence) Home schooling was forced upon us during the Covid 19 pandemic but since then it has become a growing trend. **(Research point)** The National Association of Home Schooling Society released a statement last week claiming that they urgently need resources to deal with the unexpected increase in demand for home schooling education packages post pandemic. **(My comments)** This gives us a clear indication that the movement is not a temporary move as education services have long since resumed normal service. It would appear that what was a temporary solution to a crisis has stuck! Home schooling was traditionally for those who were either unable to attend school as a result of living in a remote location; as a result of a health issue preventing them from attending mainstream education; or, as in the case of the majority, parents who simply preferred to educate their children at home. However, this is no longer the case as many more parents enthusiastically sign up, to try their hand at becoming 'teaching parents '. **(My comments)** It would appear that it is no longer considered unusual to turn your kitchen into a classroom. During lockdown, a new type of education quickly emerged: a more independent, flexible, digitally reliant sort of education and guess what? Teachers still got paid. Children were still educated. The scene was set for a radical change in the way we educate our youngsters.

(References consulted would be added to a bibliography at the end – see the essay **on 'Sgt. Pepper's Lonely Hearts Club Band'** on page 71.)

Now complete this for all of your key ideas before finally drawing a strong and opinionated conclusion.

Conclusion

In the final section of your essay, you will want come to a conclusion. Make sure you are rounding off with a strong section that brings together your key ideas. You can reflect and leave the matter unresolved, having highlighted your opinions on an important idea, or you can come to a definite conclusion. You should not rush this part. Do use persuasive techniques. Try to reference one or two key points from you main section. Ensure you are drawing one or more conclusions.

(Sample conclusion) On balance, there are plenty of arguments both for and against home schooling. However, this has surely been the case for all major changes to the education system and it is evident that for both a great many pupils, and parents, a move to a more progressive and flexible way of learning would be hugely beneficial. In recent times, the new landscape for the UK's workforce has undergone a radical transformation as a significant percentage of the population have packed up their offices in favour of the digital nomad lifestyle – working from campervans on the road or in a location of their choice. It makes sense then, to have the option of a school system that prepares us for the modern non-office based way of working. We shouldn't fear change in our education system. As a progressive and modern society, we should utterly embrace it.

Language techniques that can help your writing feel more persuasive. (The list is not exhaustive.)	How they work	Why they are persuasive
Alliteration	Use of the same letter or sound in words that are adjacent to each other. Stands out and is memorable. Draws reader's attention.	A visual reminder to the reader of your point.
Exaggeration	Over the top.	An emotive way of highlighting the point quickly – do not over use.
Use of facts	Backs up an opinion through credible research.	Makes the point reliable/believable.
Opinions	Your own beliefs. The opposite of fact! But certainly no less valid.	Shows passion, intensity and commitment.
Repetition	Same thing more than once or an idea repeated in a different way.	It stresses your point. The more your say something the stronger the emphasis.
Exaggeration or hyperbole	Over the top. An overstatement embellishing a point.	Emphasises a point in a dramatic way. Can be quite emotive.
Statistics	Usually figures, derived from the research phase.	The piece will feel more reliable and well thought out.

Language techniques that can help your writing feel more persuasive. (The list is not exhaustive.)	How they work	Why they are persuasive
Rule of **THREE**	A structure repeated three times. Provides detailed fact – emphasises and reinforces.	Draws attention. Makes it sound impressive. Comes to conclusion. Short, sharp words or phrases that when said together create a memorable, rhetorical effect, e.g. Reduce, Reuse, Recycle. Father, Son and Holy Spirit. The Good, the Bad and the Ugly.
Emotive language	Words and phrases that make the reader feel a strong feeling. Reveals the emotion that you as the writer are feeling.	Repulsive – shows outraged Delightful – shows something charming or very agreeable.
Rhetorical question	A statement more than a question. It doesn't expect an answer.	A rhetorical device that aims to question a fact in the minds of the reader.
Rebuttal or undermining an opposing opinion	Criticising the points of the other side of the argument. Contradicts other evidence.	Elevates your own position whilst putting down the other side. A well-structured argument should always contain a rebuttal.
Anecdote	A narrative or short interesting story to make a point.	Easier to understand – believable. Readers can draw comparisons.
Direct address	Directly speaks to the reader for example through the use of personal such as 'you'.	Involves the reader by making it clear that the writer is address the reader.

Assessment tool for 4th level persuasive writing

Key learning outcome	Example of success criteria	Suggestions for improvement
Is the topic for your essay original?	What are you going to argue?	Are you sure it isn't an over done topic or one that is not worthy of arguing?
Have you built a substantial convincing and effective line of thought or argument through effective research?	Have you explored 4-5 key areas in detail? Or have you tried to add too many points resulting in a lack of depth?	Don't rely on too much personal opinion, most topics require that you back up your ideas with robust research. Look for evidence which is: similar to the key points you are making; offers a slightly different perspective; anecdotal; reveals statistics; or refutes key ideas to show a more considered approach? Use linkage to build your arguments. Use effective topic sentences for each new section.
Have you planned for an effective structure?	Have you included a lively and original introduction and built a solid argument which ends with a strong conclusion?	Does your evidence build in a sensible order and appear lively and substantial? Try to show a consistent stance all the way through (unless you have introduced a counterargument)? If you writing a discursive essay have you created a balanced argument? Try to reinforce your stance in a clever way in the conclusion – perhaps returning to a point you made at the beginning, an opening statement or even the title. Try to ensure that at least one point you make in your conclusion refers back to the main part of your essay and make sure you know why?

Key learning outcome	Example of success criteria	Suggestions for improvement
Have you shown an awareness of audience and applied language techniques effectively to create tone?	Have you effectively applied techniques appropriate to the genre?	Check the previous chapter on persuasive techniques.
Have you checked and closely edited your work?	Does the technical accuracy meet the minimum standard?	Closely check spelling, punctuation, varied sentence structure, any misplaced capital letters or any unintentional repetition. It can be helpful to read your work out loud as it helps you to identify errors that you otherwise might miss. Get somebody to read over your work if this is an area that you struggle with.
Have you avoided plagiarism?	Did you include a reference section?	Make sure you acknowledge all of your references, including direct quotes and ideas that you have summarised or paraphrased from the work of others.

Please note – as with all other pieces of writing you are expected to demonstrate a **minimum standard of literacy** so edit very carefully.

What does a great essay look like?

The following article, written by a pupil from Carrick Academy in South Ayrshire, is both lively and effective. Read through the essay carefully. Then, using the assessment tool on pages 69–70, consider how the article may be said to be **original** and **effective**. You should pay careful attention to the author's line of thought (is it consistent and explored in enough depth), structure, awareness of audience and use of language techniques. If there is any language you don't understand use a dictionary to look it up.

'Sgt. Pepper's Lonely Hearts Club Band' is the Most Important Album Ever Made

It was three years ago today (give or take) that I first heard The Beatles' 'Sgt Pepper's Lonely Hearts Club Band'. I was mind-blown. For forty magical minutes I was transported into the world of four Liverpudlians with the world at their fingertips. I could barely understand it. Why was there a crowd cheering over blazing guitars and layers of horns? Who let the drummer sing? A sitar? This thing may have been about fifty years old, but it sounded like the future. However this isn't about my experience. This is about how a piece of wax changed the world. It may be clichéd nowadays, but I really think there's no denying that 'Sgt Pepper's Lonely Hearts Club Band' is the most important album ever made.

First of all, let's start with the facts, of which there are too many to go though. I could tell you that 'Pepper' is often considered to be the first 'concept' album in popular music (more on that later). I could also tell you that it is ranked number one on 'Rolling Stone' magazine's '500 Greatest Albums of All Time'. I could also mention how it was the first 'rock' album to win the Grammy for album of the year. I could go on but I have a word count to stick to.

However, despite these accolades, you cannot equate significance based on the number of awards it won. No, to judge that something is important, you must look at what it did for its respective medium in both the short and long term. And what 'Pepper' did for the album cannot be understated. 'Pepper' changed the very concept of the LP from being mere entertainment to a legitimate piece of art. The Beatles achieved this by changing the playing field completely. By taking on the guise of the fictionalised, titular band, they allowed themselves to break free from not only their own identities, but the constraints of contemporary pop music. The rules no longer mattered (or existed). With the burden of being the biggest band on the planet off their shoulders, John, Paul, George and Ringo explored musical realms that their peers could only dream of. This resulted in the first 'concept' album. The contemporary critic may argue that this is in fact false, as The Beach Boys' 'Pet Sounds', released the previous year contained songs with overarching themes, and to be fair, Frank Sinatra had been making concept albums since the late fifties. However this was the first time that the concept deeply influenced the *music*. 'Pepper' plays less like a few hit singles and a handful of filler, and more like one cohesive piece of music, much like a symphony, albeit a very trippy one. 'Pepper' revealed pop music's full potential, allowing it to become the creative and cultural force it was always meant to be.

Speaking of art, 'Pepper' changed the game not just musically, but visually as well. Art without aesthetic value is usually, rather bland, no matter how thought provoking or 'deep' it may be. Which is why 'Pepper's' cover is just as important as the music. Despite being obviously, rather beautiful, the cover goes hand in hand with the concept of the music, showcasing the band in all their colourful glory. However the cover also in a way predicted its own place in the pantheons of higher art. The inclusion of figures of both 'high culture' such as Karl Marx and Dylan Thomas, as well 'pop' icons such as Marlon Brando and Marilyn Monroe on the album cover represents the mix of high and low cultures which the Beatles achieved with the record. This furthered the idea that popular music could be appreciated as 'art'. The cover was also caused future artists to drift away from the typical 'band photo' of the era to more conceptual images that complimented the music when crafting their own album covers.

But forget all this talk about 'art'. What really makes 'Pepper' (and all great albums) so great is the quality of the songs. Taking on influences ranging from contemporary psychedelia to eastern philosophy, the Beatles expertly crafted the most vibrant and eclectic songs of their careers. Completing the departure from their early 'pop rock' sound and into the depths of modern sonic experimentation, a journey which they began on 1965's 'Rubber Soul', the albums thirteen tracks encompass a wide range of genres, from the psychedelic outing of Lennon's 'Lucy in the Sky with Diamonds' to indulgent Music hall escapades courtesy of McCartney's 'When I'm Sixty Four'. But the Beatles weren't just looking to the past and future. They were taking direct inspiration from those around them, citing the aforementioned 'Pet Sounds' as perhaps the main influence on 'Pepper'. That album's influence can be clearly heard on 'She's Leaving Home', a classically influenced piece containing both the intertwining harmonies and orchestral instrumentation that made 'Pet Sounds' such a masterpiece. The result is one of the album's peaks, with lush instrumentation, a melancholy vocal delivery, and lyrical content with a message that starkly contrasted the optimism of the era. The 'Flower Power' movement was only just beginning, but the cracks were already beginning to show. The Beatles saw through this façade and delivered a track which showcased the reality of the times. This subtle criticism would echo through the music industry during the next few years, as more and more artists began to realise that the Utopian idealism of the hippies was not all it was cracked out to be. But the Beatles were among the first to do so, giving more credit to 'Pepper's' timeless status.

Quite contrarily however, arguably 'Pepper's' most important song is one that embraces this doctrine. George Harrison's 'Within You Without You' is a far cry from the typical pop song of the era. In fact it was hardly a pop song at all. A spiritual journey which completely contradicts anything 'She's leaving Home' had to say about the times. The track in fact had a profound influence on the hippie movement, by bringing into focus eastern philosophies of peace and understanding, which helped fuel the movement and perhaps give it some weight. But it wasn't just the ideology that makes 'Within You Without You' so important. It was the style. The song is essentially a piece of Indian classical music with a pop melody on top. Sure, Harrison had tackled Indian music before, on 'Revolver's' 'Love You To', released the previous year. But he was only flirting. This track is a full on odyssey, complete with a classical Indian backing band. The fact that a band of this magnitude released a song like this had a tremendous effect on what was considered suitable for inclusion on a pop album. Not only did it bring Indian music to the masses, it also encouraged others to indulge in other forms of world music, giving a breath of fresh air from the western dominated musical landscape of the time.

Hype is a horrible thing. Hype can cause confusion. Hype can cause disappointment. When something is as acclaimed as 'Pepper', there is really no way to hear it objectively. Listened to with modern ears, 'Pepper' can feel formulaic, pedestrian, or just plain boring. I personally couldn't understand this until I recently played the album for some friends after explaining its brilliance to them - they could hardly sit through it. But I made the mistake of trying to tell them why they should have loved it, rather than letting the album do the talking. I suppose that revelation is rather ironic, considering the article I have just written. But it doesn't matter. Because sometimes the hype is right. Sometimes it is right to describe something as being 'mind-blowing' or 'life-changing'. 'Pepper' changed music but it also changed lives. It certainly changed mine.

Author Brad Gibson

Bibliography

www.pitchfork.com

www.rollingstone.com

www.absoluteradio.co.uk

www.officialcharts.com

www.newseek.com

www.lifezette.com

https://www.youtube.com/watch?v=_st4diqjpis

'I Just Wasn't Made For These Times' – Charles L.Granata

Further practice

Creating news content

There are a number of expectations that you will have to consider when creating a news article. Both layout and content are important – have a look at any newspaper or magazine article to illustrate this. Generally, in a printed news article, you would expect to find: a **heading**; a **byline** (to reveal the author and often the location); the **lead paragraph** and **supporting paragraphs**.

1. Headline

Your headline will be very dependent on the type of paper you choose to write for (see News Article chapter for examples) if you are writing for a tabloid newspaper you may want to use a pun in your headline. This is your **hook** so try to be creative.

Task 23

Research and make a list of some famous tabloid `puns'. Many of them caused scandal. Now consider as many recent news stories as you can and try to make up some sensationalist headlines of your own.

2. Lead paragraph

This is found at the beginning of the article and will be a summary of the whole of the article. This will become your plan as you will simply expand upon each section in the rest of your article. It must be short and succinct. This is where you will want to answer the questions of: **who**: (who is involved in the story); **what** (what is the point of interest of the story); **when** (did the event happen); **where** (the main location); **why** (the motive or background surrounding the story) and **how** the events unfolded.

3. Supporting paragraphs

This is where you expand on each of the above sections. You will expand using quotes, explanation and details. Remember, if you are writing for a tabloid newspaper to include opinion and **'spin'**.

Headline	
Photo	
Lead paragraph: **Who?** **What?** **When?** **Where?** **Why?** **How?** Supporting paragraphs will start here, expanding on the above key points and extend into the next column.	Continue your supporting paragraphs **here**. Don't forget that no matter which newspaper type you choose, your language must be effective, your writing succinct and, as always you must edit your work so that you are meeting the standard for literacy.

What makes a good news story?

Use this checklist to help you decide.

1. Remember to focus on the **purpose** of your article – you must engage your audience so think about what may make them interested.

2. **Timing** – is this old news? If so, move on -unless you have a very original slant.

3. **Significance** – try to choose a trending issue or 'hot topic' (good for magazine articles) or a local issue – good for local press publications as you hope the audience will be invested. People who write on social media platforms will research the number of times a particular topic has been researched to find out whether there will be enough interest for the topic they have chosen. It needs to be very significant to a number of people, not just you. Remember that you should be using **emotive language** to bring a more human element and make it feels less detached.

4. Think about the **information** you have – is it original have you thought of a new angle or have you found out something new?

5. **Consequence** – who would be (or has been) affected by the issue and how?

6. **Relevance** – why is your article relevant? Why will your audience want to (or need to know)?

Where to look for news ideas

Social media feeds (both local, national and international); news programs both online and in print; other magazine articles; and by talking to people. Think about what people talking about and about what interests your target audience.

TIP: for ethical news reporting check the IPSO code of conduct. They decide what you can and cannot say and if you were a journalist breaking the rules would have serious consequences. https://www.ipso.co.uk/editors-code-of-practice

Glossary and Answers

Glossary

Word – Definition

Abstract – something that is more an idea than a solid object. Feelings can be considered abstract.

Affiliate link – a specific URL that contains the affiliate's ID, which links to a product or service, often for financial gain and often hidden within content.

Anecdotal evidence – relatable or relevant stories told about something that has happened to the speaker or to someone else. Subjective and not based on fact.

Antagonist – the main villain of the story.

Atmosphere or mood – a sense of, for example, fear or drama.

Biased – when something is supported or opposed in an unfair or unbalanced way as a result of allowing personal opinions to influence content or decisions.

Characterisation – the representations of characters in a text that bring them to life.

Connotation – the ideas or qualities evoked by a word or phrase.

Context – the details that give a frame of reference to a story. Context helps us to better understand the full picture.

Denotation – the widely agreed meaning of a word, such as you may find in a dictionary.

Dialogue – verbal and non-verbal communication between characters.

Dramatic monologue – a piece of writing or a speech that presents the thoughts of just one character to the audience.

Fake news – false or misleading content presented as fact. The purpose is often to sell something or to damage the reputation of an institution or person.

Genre – types of texts that can be grouped together as they share similar traits.

Hook – the start of a piece of writing aimed at piquing the curiosity of the reader and making them want to read on.

Imagery – a visually descriptive representation of something. Imagery helps to form a clear picture in the mind of the reader.

Imaginative – something that is creative. This can relate to both fiction and non-fiction writing.

Impartiality – unbiased. Treating or presening something fairly or equally.

Language – in terms of writing, 'language' refers to the use of language (e.g. use of imagery, word choice, sentence structure, etc.).

Metaphor – an expression that describes something by referring to something else which is the same in a particular way. For example, if you want to say that someone is very shy and frightened of things, you might say that they are a mouse.

Monologue – a long speech (or piece of writing) that presents the thoughts of one character.

Mood – in terms of writing, 'mood' refers to the 'atmosphere' or 'tone' of the writing.

Narration style – the way a story is told.

Narrative structure – the way a story is put together. The start and end of the story and the order of everything in between.

Narrator – the 'voice' that tells the story. This could be a story told from a character's perspective (first person narrative), or from a voice not connected to the story (third person narrative).

Plot – storyline.

Premise – a brief statement of the idea of a story.

Protagonist – the main character (or hero) of a story.

Pun – a play on words (e.g. as used in some newspaper headlines).

Rhetoric – the exploitation of language to create a persuasive effect.

Setting – the time and place in which a story is set.

Simile – a device used by a writer to show that something in the text is comparable to (or 'like') something else.

Spin – a deliberate angle on a news story to meet a specific purpose (e.g. to entertain).

Structure – the order in which a story is put together.

Theme – a key idea explored in a text.

Answers

TASK 4:

2. a) This is a genre that you may be unfamiliar with although it is commonly used by pupils. It belongs to the **social realism** genre.

   b) Should be easily recognisable from the **suspense** genre.

TASK 11:

- Albert planted the forest.
- My sister Orla gave me the ring.
- Autumn poured the drinks.
- Callum and Leon threw the bricks that broke the windows.
- Iona won the race.

ebook

To access the ebook version, visit collins.co.uk/ebooks and follow the step-by-step instructions.